A Time for Healing: Coming to Terms with Your Divorce

HAROLD IVAN SMITH

LifeWay Press
Nashville, Tennessee

ACKNOWLEDGEMENTS

A Time for Healing: Coming to Terms with Your Divorce
Copyright © 1994 by LifeWay Press
Fifth printing September 2002

ISBN 0-8054-9875-3
Dewey Decimal Number 306.89
Subject Heading: DIVORCE

Sources for definitions in a *Time for Healing: Coming to Terms with Your Divorce*
By permission. From *Webster's Ninth New Collegiate Dictionary* © 1991 by Merriam-Webster Inc., publisher of the Meriam-Webster.

Unless otherwise indicated, biblical quotations are from the Holy Bible, *New International Version*, copyright © 1973, 1978, 1984 by International Bible Society (NIV). Other versions used: *New American Standard Bible.* © The Lockman Foundation, 1960, 1962, 1963, 1968, 1971, 1972, 1973, 1975, 1977. Used by permission; the *Revised Standard Version* (RSV) © 1946 (New Testament), and © 1952 (Old Testament) by Division of Christian Education of the National Council of Churches of Christ in the United States of America; the *King James Version* (KJV).

To order additional copies of this resource:

- WRITE LifeWay Church Resources Customer Service
  One LifeWay Plaza
  Nashville, TN 37234-0113
- FAX order to (615) 251-5933
- PHONE (800) 458-2772
- EMAIL to *CustomerService@lifeway.com*
- ORDER ONLINE at *www.lifeway.com*; or
- VISIT the LifeWay Christian Store serving you.

Printed in the United States of America

Adult Ministry Publishing
LifeWay Church Resources
One LifeWay Plaza
Nashville, TN 37234-0175

Table of Contents

About the Author

Harold Ivan Smith, a nationally known speaker on issues pertaining to single adults, is president of Harold Ivan Smith and Associates, a consulting firm in Kansas City, Missouri. He received the doctor of ministry degree from Asbury Theological Seminary in 1993 and the doctor of ministry degree from Luther Rice Seminary in 1985.

Himself a single adult, Smith has written such books as *51 Good Things to Do While You're Waiting for the Right One to Come Along*; *Reluctantly Single*; and *I Wish Someone Understood My Divorce*; and under the pen name of Jason Towner wrote *Jason Loves Jane* and *Warm Reflections* about the experience of his own divorce.

LIFE® Support Group Series Editorial Team
Kay Moore, Design Editor
Dale McCleskey, Editor
Kenny Adams, Manuscript Assistant

Graphics by Lori Putnam
Cover Design by Edward Crawford

The Agendas of Recovery

> ## FEELING DEFEATED AND HOPELESS
>
> Kevin's wife left him for his best friend. Two years later, Kevin is still cynical and bitter. At first, after the divorce, his friends tried to support him by inviting him to go places with them, but Kevin refused their invitations. After numerous rejections, his friends took the hint and left Kevin alone. Now, Kevin is pretty much of a loner. When he's not working at his job, he keeps to himself and doesn't often venture from his home. Kevin still lives in the same house where he and Andrea lived when they were married. Family members have suggested that he move to a new location to gain a new perspective, but Kevin refuses to explore any options. Angry because he believes that God did not act to prevent his divorce, Kevin also has rejected his faith. Friends have invited him to attend the singles group at a nearby church, but Kevin believes that his faith is useless to him now in the wake of this devastating event in his marriage. Feeling defeated and hopeless, Kevin has all but given up on life.

Many of us can identify with Kevin because of the hopelessness that we have felt about the dissolution of our marriages. Divorce is a horrifying experience that can cause us to feel that everything in our lives is becoming unhinged. Because he has allowed these circumstances to thoroughly devastate him, however, Kevin is having an unhealthy reaction that could cause him to sustain much emotional, spiritual, and even physical harm.

If Kevin continues on his present course, he will shut himself off from the fellowship of all those who try to help him. He will not take advantage of the hope and healing that can occur by leaning on God as his source of strength. His depression could affect him physically if he refuses to seek healthy outlets for his stress. His reaction even could affect his employment if his hopeless attitude about life keeps him from doing his best at work.

A Time for Healing: Coming to Terms with Your Divorce would help Kevin take some positive steps toward recovering from his divorce. It would help him realize that rather than being buffeted by life's circumstances, Kevin has the power, through Christ, to make decisions that will determine how his divorce affects his future. He can learn to deal with the agendas—or the groups of decisions—that can move him toward healing.

In *A Time for Healing* you will take these steps to change present behavior:
• Learn to view your divorce as a process, rather than a one-time event that you can get over and move beyond quickly;
• Learn to intentionally relinquish some attachments to relationships that are linked to the marriage;
• Learn some new ways of responding to people and to situations;
• Gain insight into daily survival and coping skills;

What's in it for you

- Learn how to recognize counterfeit relationships and learn how premature relationships can short-circuit your recovery;
- Explore your future as a divorced individual and learn how God can help you in that future.

For example, instead of isolating himself to keep from being hurt again, Kevin can choose to be around certain friends who will affirm him yet be honest with him. Instead of rejecting his faith, Kevin can be reminded that God partners with the wounded and dispenses blessings in the midst of life's unfairness. Kevin can learn to forgive himself and others so that old hurt and bitterness will not continue to hold him back from a productive, abundant life.

On the inside back cover you will find an illustration of the agendas of divorce recovery, which you will study in *A Time for Healing.* This illustration will help you visualize where you are going on this journey.

How this course fits in

A Time for Healing: Coming to Terms with Your Divorce is part of the LIFE® Support Group Series, an educational system of discovery-group and support-group resources for providing Christian ministry and emotional support to individuals in areas of social, emotional, and physical need. These resources deal with such life issues as chemical dependency, codependency, abuse recovery, eating disorders, divorce, and grieving life's losses. Individuals using LIFE® Support Group Series courses will be led through recovery to discipleship and ministry.

A Time for Healing is a support-group course designed to be basic to any church's support-group ministry. A support group studies dysfunctional family issues and other sensitive emotional issues that individuals might face. A carefully selected group facilitator guides discussion of the topics and helps group members process what they have learned during their study. This group is not a therapy group. Rather, this is a self-help group, in which group members help each other by talking in a safe, loving environment.

A Time for Healing is an integrated course of study. To achieve the full benefit of the educational design, prepare your individual assignments, and participate in the group sessions.

To achieve the greatest benefit from this course, ask your church to schedule this course for the full nine sessions that this workbook includes. However, for churches that believe they can offer only an abbreviated schedule to accommodate the often pressured life situations of people experiencing or those who have experienced divorce, the first six sessions represent the core agendas of *A Time for Healing,* and the last three sessions are optional. Your church may add any or all of the last three that time will allow.

How to study the book

Study Tips. Five days a week (which compose a unit, or an "agenda") you will be expected to study a segment of content material. You may need from 30 to 60 minutes of study time each day. Even if you find that you can study the material in less time, spread out the study over five days. This will give you more time to apply the truths to your life. Study at your own pace. Study the material as if Harold Ivan Smith is sitting at your side helping you learn. When the book asks you a question or gives you an assignment, respond immediately. Each assignment is indented and appears in **boldface type.** When we ask you to respond in writing, a pencil appears beside the assignment. For example, an assignment will look like the one that follows:

✎ **Read Psalm 139:13. Write what the verse tells about God's care for you.**

In an actual activity, a line would appear below each assignment. You would write your answer on this line. When we ask you to respond in a nonwriting manner—for example, by thinking about or praying about a matter—an arrow appears beside the assignment. This type of assignment will look like this:

⫸ **Stop and pray, thanking God for being with you during painful times.**

In most cases your "personal tutor" will give you some feedback about your response—for example, a suggestion about what you might have written. Set a definite time and select a quiet place where you can study with little interruption. Keep a Bible handy for times when the material asks you to look up Scripture. Memorizing Scripture is an important part of your work.

Getting the most from the course

Support-Group Session. Once each week, attend an *A Time for Healing* support-group session designed to help members discuss the content they studied the previous week and share personal responses to issues and problems. These groups provide a safe and loving environment for personal and spiritual healing, growth, and recovery.

The support group adds a needed dimension to your learning. If you are not involved in a group study, try to enlist some friends or associates who have experienced or are experiencing divorce and who will work through this course with you. Approach your church leaders about beginning such a group. *A Time for Healing Facilitator's Guide* (0805498761) provides guidance and learning activities for these sessions. (For orders or inquiries WRITE LifeWay Church Resources Customer Service, 127 Ninth Avenue, North, Nashville, TN 37234-0113; FAX order to (615) 251-5933; PHONE 1-800-458-2772; EMAIL to *CustomerService@lifeway.com*; ONLINE at *www.lifeway.com*; or visit the LifeWay Christian Store serving you.) Your church also may want to children affected by their parents' divorce. *KidShare: What Do I Do Now?* (0805498877) and the facilitator guide provides resources for these age groups.

A key decision

A Time for Healing is written with the assumption that you already have received Jesus Christ as your Savior and that you have Him guiding you in the healing process. If you have not yet made the crucial decision to receive Christ, you will find in Agenda 4 guidance for how to do so. You will benefit more from *A Time for Healing* if you have Jesus working in and guiding your life. Many people can testify that in the rubble of a divorce they found Jesus to be their friend. Allow Jesus to work in your life during this time of recovery.

A large number of divorced or divorcing persons are casualties of infidelity, abandonment, abuse, and other circumstances destructive to a covenantal relationship. The recovery process this course outlines affirms God's laws regarding marriage, divorce, and remarriage. Some individuals are not free to marry again from a biblical perspective (see Agenda 9, "Some Biblical Dimensions.") Participants who find themselves unable or unwilling to follow the biblical guidelines on which this healing process is based should seek help from a pastor or Christian counselor. *A Time for Healing* is not about assessing blame but is about accepting responsibility and celebrating the grace of God who offers healing, forgiveness, and hope to all. May this be the time for your healing!

Viewing Your Divorce as a Process

This week's agenda:
You will recognize your divorce as a process rather than an event.

WOUNDS FROM THE PAST

Laura caught her husband with another woman in Laura's own bedroom—a room Laura had carefully decorated and furnished. After her husband moved out, Laura continued to sleep in that bedroom—or at least she tried to sleep there. Often she slowly replayed the discovery in her mind.

Alan, divorced after 20 years of marriage, loved giving cards and gifts—particularly surprises—to his wife. Now, when he finds himself having to buy a card, he immediately wanders to the cards in the "sweetheart" section, especially at Christmas, Easter, Valentine's, and even on no-reason occasions. He reads the cards, thinking, "If only we were still married . . .." He looks at cards and becomes depressed.

What do Laura and Alan need in their lives? On page 16 you will read more about their situations.

What you'll learn

This week you will—
- recognize divorce as a process leading either to a false healing or to genuine recovery;
- identify three types of divorced people;
- recognize the difference between wounds and scars;
- review the path to divorce and to recovery;
- become acquainted with the agendas of divorce recovery.

What you'll study

A Process, Not an Event	Types of Divorced People	Recognizing Wounds and Scars	Discovering Paths to Recovery	Learning Recovery Agendas
DAY 1	DAY 2	DAY 3	DAY 4	DAY 5

Memory verse

This week's verse of Scripture to memorize—
For I am the Lord, your God, who takes hold of your right hand and says to you, "Do not fear; I will help you."

—Isaiah 41:13

DAY 1

Today's objective:
You will recognize fully your divorce as a process rather than an event.

Your direction—toward recovery

A Process, Not an Event

Admitting that Life Has Changed

The scenario goes like this: a riot or mini revolution breaks out in some foreign country. Immediately the U.S. State Department swings into action to determine who or what is the legitimate government. Sometimes, after days or weeks, the State Department reluctantly must "recognize" or admit the existence of the new government, sometimes even when the new government contradicts the interests of the United States and the concept of democracy. To recognize is to formally acknowledge something exists even if you don't want it to exist.

In today's lesson we will discuss a commitment to recognize fully the reality of your divorce and to recognize divorce as a process, not simply an event.

For some people this will mean three steps forward and two steps back. You may have patted yourself on the back for how well you're dealing with the divorce, as you juggle your physical, financial, emotional, and spiritual survival. Then, like a character in an old Western movie waiting for the stagecoach bearing the gold shipment, you were ambushed! Bang! Boom! Zonk! You may have felt yourself back at square one. Fresh tears, fresh wounds.

The process of divorce involves movement—forward and backward. This process is not a smooth path. It does not progress along a straight line, although some people pretend it does. Rather, it is like a mountain road—lots of right turns, left turns, and an occasional "you can't get there from here."

For some people, healing has been delayed and even complicated by poor, hasty decisions in the early hours, days, or weeks of a divorce, especially when a person did not expect the divorce to occur.

✎ **Place a check by the following "early" decisions which either complicated your divorce or are delaying recovery from the divorce:**
❏ Spouse changed life insurance policies.
❏ I changed life insurance policies.
❏ Spouse diverted funds to secret bank accounts.
❏ I diverted funds to secret bank accounts.
❏ Spouse abused credit cards.
❏ I abused credit cards.
❏ Spouse canceled credit cards.
❏ I canceled credit cards.
❏ Spouse changed titles on assets.
❏ I changed titles on assets.
❏ Spouse interfered with access to children.
❏ I interfered with access to children.
❏ Spouse sabotaged children's affection.
❏ I sabotaged children's affection.
❏ Spouse raided savings account.
❏ I raided savings account.
❏ Spouse emptied joint checking account.
❏ I emptied joint checking account.

❑ Spouse _____

❑ I _____

Often, the initiator already has become accustomed to the idea of a divorce before he or she told the spouse. So, while one spouse is saying, "This can't be happening to us/me!" the other spouse is scripting the next act, which could mean the next indignity or at least choosing the next field of conflict: child custody, loyalty of friends, or property settlement.

Ignoring reality

Some well-meaning Christians have set themselves up for the proverbial trip "to the cleaners" by denying that the process is significant. No matter how loudly or with what intensity you declare, "This isn't happening to me!" you are ignoring reality. Yes, it is happening, or yes, it has happened, to you.

The Haste Hazard

Recovery also requires time—lots of time, a commodity many divorced people are reluctant to give, especially since a potential new spouse can be waiting in the wings (or sometimes in the hallway outside the courtroom). Our society has become so accustomed to divorce that it counsels, "You'll get over it." Given the American tendency to impatience, people want you to get over a divorce immediately; people encouraged you right away to start dating or "to get out some" or "go meet some new people." American society says, "Life goes on."

Early advice

✎ **Think a moment and recall some of the early advice people gave you. Jot down some "tidbits" that come to mind.**

_____

Did you receive some advice you now wish you had followed?

_____

Did you receive advice you now wish you had not followed?

_____

For example, you might have written something like this: "People advised me to move to another town so I could 'get over it' more quickly. I followed that advice and now wish I hadn't acted so hastily. People advised me to continue attending church after my separation. I stopped going to church because I thought I couldn't face people. Now I realize how much I needed the support of my church and wish I had followed the advice."

Historically, the state and the church agreed on lengthy divorce processes to discourage divorce or to give time for all parties involved to think through the process. This lengthy process was one reason for American colonists' "thirst" for independence from England. In the 1700's, the couple or individual wishing to divorce first had to go to the Church of England and petition for divorce. The petitioner had to prove that the spouse had broken the bonds of the marriage. Most often the petitioner proved that the spouse committed adultery. If the church gave an ecclesiastical divorce, the petitioner went to Parliament and asked for a "bill of divorce" to be introduced. Divorce was costly, complicated, and long.

However, colonists who wanted a divorce had to go back to England and thus were away from the lands, or plantations, or businesses, for perhaps a year. So, the colonies began setting up colonial divorces. An outraged George III in 1774 declared all the divorces granted in the colonies void.[1] After the Revolution, divorce law was expedited. Divorce became a matter for civil authorities. Eventually, some cash-hungry states and Caribbean nations saw a lucrative market for those who didn't have time to wait; they set up "quickie" divorces. In Nevada, someone could take up residence for six weeks, work on his or her tan, be only slightly inconvenienced by a brief courtroom appearance, and the divorce could be settled. Indeed, rent-a-preachers and tiny wedding chapels sprang up to provide speedy second marriages before a person left town.

Time for Positive Healing

No time for mourning

Time spent in the divorce process provides for healing. Sadly, many people fast-forward over the opportunities for positive healing. Some people do not schedule any time for mourning. We cannot accomplish recovery without discomfort—even pain. Some deliberately make choices to avoid the painful work of healing. Some seem to think that a speedy second marriage or a live-in relationship proves that a person is over a divorce.

Weekly Work

➠ **Begin to memorize this week's memory verse, Isaiah 41:13.**

✎ **Some divorced people testify that God has taken their hand and led them through the dangerous intersections of the divorce process. Below write one way you now can see that God is helping you through this divorce and toward recovery.**

_____

Divorce is a process, not simply an event for me. I will give myself time to heal.

What prevented you from recognizing God's hand earlier?

_____

➠ **Say aloud the affirmation appearing in the margin.**

DAY 2

Today's objective:
You will identify three types of divorced people.

Types of Divorced People

Choosing How to Respond

Early in my separation a minister offered me some key wisdom: *What matters is not so much what happens to you but rather how you choose to respond.* You may not have chosen this separation/divorce, BUT you do choose how you respond to it.

You can sabotage your recovery in hundreds of ways. Consider the activity that appears on the next page.

✎ **Check the responses that most accurately identify your choices.**

1. ❏ I responded actively to my divorce/ ❏ I responded passively to my divorce.
2. ❏ I based my responses on need/ ❏ I based my responses on fault.
3. ❏ I negotiated with my spouse in good faith/ ❏ I negotiated with my spouse in bad faith.
4. ❏ I expressed my anger./ ❏ I repressed my anger.
5. ❏ I dealt honestly with my anger./ ❏ I substituted negative behavior instead of dealing honestly with my anger.
6. ❏ I accepted responsibility./ ❏ I assigned blame.

If you checked responses in the second group of statements, you probably have delayed your recovery.

In his book, *The On Purpose Person*, Kevin McCarthy urges readers to live a life with purpose, regardless of what life dishes out. Using a river as an analogy for life, he identifies three types of individuals: floaters, fighters, and navigators. I believe his categories apply to divorced or divorcing people, too.

✎ **Without skipping ahead, take a moment to guess what characterizes the classifications of floaters, fighters, and navigators. As you read the descriptions below, put a check mark in the margin beside the category that you think characterizes you at the time of your divorce or when you learned you would be divorcing; put an * in the margin beside the category that best characterizes you now.**

Floaters

"Floaters passively resign themselves to accept the river (the divorce) . . . they aimlessly go along for the ride"[2] whichever direction the river takes. Floaters, in divorcing, find themselves living out the pattern of their marriage. For example, they may have been passively married and may have found themselves saying, "Anything you say, dear." Passivity probably contributed to some of the dynamics that led to, or at least influenced, the divorce.

"Why bother?"

Even though some couples act violently as they go through divorce, the Floater hardly responds to the process. The Floater may argue that he/she can do nothing to change the mind of the initiator of the divorce, so why bother? The Floater almost prides himself/herself on the unmessiness of the divorce. No angry scenes. Many of these individuals were reared in homes where they were taught not to feel, not to vocalize one's pain, and not to create scenes.

Floaters believe that since they are not the initiators of the situation, they do not need to take any action to make their circumstances better. They believe that since they are victims, they do not need to do anything to help their situation. Therefore they merely float along, buffeted by the tides of life's circumstances that surround them. Floaters behave passively and seem to invite others to rescue them from distress. Often no shortage of volunteers exists willing to rescue them, including lawyers who charge by the hour.

You have heard that it was said, "An eye for an eye, and a tooth for a tooth." But I tell you, Do not resist an evil person. If someone strikes you on the right cheek, turn to him the other also. And if someone wants to sue you and take your tunic, let him have your cloak as well. If someone forces you to go one mile, go with him two miles.

–Matthew 5:38-41

Some floaters back up their actions by modifying Jesus' words, "If your ex slaps you, turn your other cheek." Indeed, in some cases floaters don't simply desire to be perceived as religious but also desire to be "nice." This might be a good point to take a look at Jesus' words on "an eye for an eye" in Matthew 5:38-41 appearing at left. Could the statement "sue you and take your tunic" also apply to your house, your boat, or half of your retirement?

✎ **Would Jesus suggest that the divorced person go the extra mile? Take a moment and reflect on this passage. Below write what you believe are the implications of Jesus' words.**

_____

_____

How could someone take this passage to the extreme?

_____

_____

One person gave this answer: _Jesus was speaking to people whose first instinct was to fight and to hate. He said we were to overcome the urge to retaliate by responding with active love. He did not endorse passive surrender to the circumstances of life._

Fighters

I once spent a pleasant May afternoon canoeing down the Turkey Run River in central Indiana. Some fellow canoeists began discovering auxiliary uses of the paddle—specifically to splash water on other canoeists. I certainly didn't start this activity, but once someone did, I discovered I could splash water with the best of them.

Soon I was having to flail as well as bail, on my right as well as on my left, as the water in my canoe rose over my ankles. I spent a lot of time going in circles. The water others splashed in my face blinded me.

So it is with the divorce. Someone encourages us to take up the gauntlet and declare, "Two can play this game!" or, "Oh, so you want to play rough!" Suddenly, we toss aside the rules of engagement, and a brawl is on. Any arena will do for a skirmish: church, a school event, a PTA meeting, a family Christmas gathering, a chance encounter in the mall, or a soccer game. The briefest telephone conversation erupts into a shouting match or a string of accusations and threats.

Indeed, some ex-spouses are "itching" for a fight. They constantly toss out the dares: "I dare you to cross this line and see what happens." Not all fighting is physical. Some of the most permanent wounds are emotional. One can bruise the soul and never discolor the skin.

Sadly, fighters often enlist allies in the battle. Fighters may recruit family members; even children, friends, co-workers, pastors, or neighbors join the fight, or at least to provide valuable intelligence which they may use to strengthen their position against the ex. Some fighters are extremely good with labels and insults that ricochet through the canyons of the heart long after the arguing has ended. Fighters often hurl comments like,"You're so stupid!!!"; "Well, if you're so smart, how come . . .?"; "Who would ever want you?!"; "What about the time I . . .?"

Some people delight in provoking the fight. Some want to win every argument. Sometimes the only wise decision is to walk away. That is difficult for some of us to do because we feel like we are being put down; we feel like

A brawl is on

we are wimping out. A family member or friend may challenge us: "Don't let her/him get away with that . . ." or "I wouldn't stand for that if I were you . . ." or "He's making a fool of you!"

The only people who profit from fighting are the lawyers; some lawyers will prod the divorcing into skirmishes. Indeed, lawyers may be like hired "seconds" in dueling matches. What many of us want when we hire an attorney is someone who will strike fear in the heart of our ex and his/her attorney. We want to retain an attorney who knows how to file motions and petitions with such speed as to befuddle our ex and perhaps even "bring 'em to their knees." Some divorce attorneys would use the phrase "killer" in their ads if the Yellow Pages would allow it. Indeed, many divorced people long after their divorce have realized how their attorneys manipulated them. Sadly, for some, no issue is too small to fight over.

For some, no issue is too small to fight over.

✏️ **Fill in the blanks below with your responses.**

_____ is something I now wish we had not fought over.

What fueled the fight? _____

_____

Navigators

Navigators, in McCarthy's words, realize they cannot "control" the river or perhaps the particular section of the river.[3] For example, when I white-water rafted the Chatooga River in northern Georgia, I discovered some very calm sections of that river. Then with little warning, I could round a twist in the river and find myself rushing into roaring rapids.

Equipping themselves for the challenge

Navigators realize that although they did not choose the divorce, they now are in the process, so they try to equip themselves adequately for the challenge. Navigators accept the reality of divorce as a process and find ways to make the most of the "opportunities" as well as to survive the crises and ambushes.

Navigators rarely want the divorce. But once the process started, they buckle their seat belts and yell, "Hang on . . . I can cope with this." During one hot July afternoon on the Chatooga, an experienced park ranger captained our raft. We had been floating calmly for a while, but I noticed that he was looking ahead anticipating what was about to occur. I never will forget his tone of voice when he said, "OK, boys and girls, get ready." Suddenly all I could see was whitewater, rising fast. We were in the whitewater—big time. We survived because we had a good navigator and because we listened to the commands he yelled out to us.

More than one million people went through divorce the year you were divorced. But how many of them could say they have "recovered"? Did they make choices—go back to the activity on page 9 of day 1—which preempted or delayed or perhaps even indefinitely postponed healing? That's why one of the healthiest choices you have ever made is to take part in this group. Group participation will aid you in healthy decision making and will help you avoid becoming a "floater" or a "fighter."

Take a moment and decide which of these three categories has been your track record. Were you a floater, fighter, or navigator—

during separation? _____
at the time of your divorce? _____
since your divorce? _____

As a result of this section, do you need to change categories? You may have been a FLOATER or FIGHTER in all of the above categories, but the good news is that through God's grace, FIGHTERS and FLOATERS can become NAVIGATORS!

Weekly Work

 Continue to memorize this week's memory verse, Isaiah 41:13. Write it three times in the margin at the top left.

▮▶ Repeat the affirmation appearing in the margin.

Recognizing Wounds and Scars

Ever have a wound that's in the process of healing? Think about what happens when that wound gets bumped or when something irritating comes into contact with it. All the progress that's been made in healing receives a major setback.

Often, after that happens, we end up with an injury that's even more painful than the original one was. We'll learn some things about wounding rather than healing that relate to recovery from divorce.

1. Wounds require your cooperation in order to heal.

Adults who say to children, "That wound never will heal if you keep picking at it! You'll never have a chance for a scar to form" often have the most amazing inclination to reactivate emotional wounds, five miles down. These are wounds that others may not even see—wounds that draw our attention more readily than do visible injuries. Some of these are—
• "If-only" wounds: "If only I had said/done . . . "
• "I-should-have" wounds: "I should have gone for counseling. . . "
• Evidential wounds: Finding your spouse in bed with another person

 What wound repeatedly announces its presence in your life? Why can't you let go of it? Below write your response.

_____

_____

Sadly, like a three-ring circus, some divorced people are still in the wound ring one, five, ten years after the divorce.

Margin (left side):

Divorce is a process, not simply an event for me. I will give myself time to heal. I may have been a floater/fighter in the past, but with God's help I can become a NAVIGATOR!

DAY 3

Today's objective:
You will learn to recognize the difference between wounds and scars.

I'll tell one of my scar-delaying habits. When I first went through my divorce, I pored over our wedding album. I methodically examined the pictures. We were s-o-o happy then, I told myself. Yet, it was a bittersweet experience. Seventeen years after my divorce I still have that album, although I do not look through it. Some divorced people have particular places they go to dwell on their emotional wounds. Sally, for instance, goes to "their" favorite restaurant and drinks endless cups of coffee as she remembers (let's call it what it is—reopening old wounds.)

✎ **Where/when do you go to reopen emotional wounds?**

1._____ 2. _____

I'd offer Laura this advice:

_____

_____

_____

_____

Laura caught her husband with another woman in Laura's own bedroom—a room Laura had carefully decorated and furnished. After he moved out, Laura continued to sleep in that bedroom—or at least tried to sleep in that bedroom. Often she slowly replayed the discovery in her mind. In the margin write what advice you would offer Laura.

But we find more to Laura's story: One night about 2 a.m., she had a startling idea—to create a new bedroom downstairs. She began designing the new bedroom in her head and began thinking of some strong friends who would help her move the furniture. Still she did not get to sleep. At 3 a.m., Laura jumped out of bed, jerked off all the bed covers, and began lugging at the mattress. She pulled it across the room to the door and slowly began getting the mattress to the stairs. With an incredible amount of adrenaline rushing through her, she wrestled it downstairs into what had been a dining room and began creating her new bedroom. By 6 a.m., most of the drawers from the chests were downstairs. Once in that new bedroom, she declared it off-limits to dwelling on the past.

Alan, divorced after 20 years of marriage, loved giving cards and gifts—particularly surprises—to his wife. Now, when he finds himself having to buy a card, he wanders to the cards in the "sweetheart" section. He reads the cards and thinks, "If only we were still married . . . ." This generally causes him to become depressed. In the margin write what advice you'd give Alan.

I'd offer Alan this advice:

_____

_____

_____

_____

Laura's arena was a bedroom and Alan's is a card store. What is your arena? Wounds only heal with your full cooperation! If you are on a diet, you don't go into a bakery just to see what's for sale there. Avoid places that keep your emotional wounds from healing.

2. Scars eventually occur if we leave wounds alone.

The next time you're tempted to dwell on your emotional wounds, ask yourself: Do I realize that by this choice I am delaying my healing? (Sometimes we may think of the word *scar* as having a negative connotation, but when we talk about a scar in the context of divorce recovery, we're referring to a healed injury that is not vulnerable to being reopened.)

3. Stop rehearsing your wounds.

Like old war veterans

Some divorced people throw pity parties. Sometimes, divorced people are like old war veterans gathering to remember the Big One. Certainly at proper times the recovery process encourages storytelling and celebrating growth, but sometimes we decide we're "all talked out" on the subject of divorce. Next subject, please.

Sadly, we can try to one-up any divorce story. After you share a few details of your divorce, someone smirks, "Oh, you had it easy. You want to hear about divorce? I'll tell you about divorce . . .." Some divorced people conclude that constantly rehearsing—or rehashing—our divorce epics tie us to the past and do not lead us into the future to which God is calling.

4. Invite Jesus to become Lord of your wounds.

Moments will occur when the path of least resistance leads to a good "woe-is-me" party with you at the head table. Sometimes counselors prod, "What are you gaining by dwelling on this/these wounds?" Sympathy? Pity? Escape from responsibility? In the early days of your separation/divorce, that may have been necessary, but now?

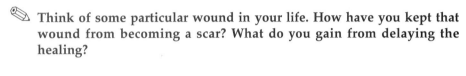 **Think of some particular wound in your life. How have you kept that wound from becoming a scar? What do you gain from delaying the healing?**

_____

_____

The movie _Shadowlands_ depicts the brief marriage of C. S. Lewis, a confirmed bachelor with strong feelings against divorce. He marries Joy, a divorced woman with two children. Joy had cancer when he married her. Lewis—a great Oxford poet and Christian apologist—faced his own front-and-center personal agony while she was alive and his own grief after she died. The believer who had written bestseller _The Problem of Pain_ struggled to answer his own intense questions about suffering—this time not from the comfort of his Oxford ivory tower but from his own small slice of hell. Reflect on a passage in Lewis' writing of this period: "We want to prove to ourselves that we are lovers on the grand scale, tragic, heroes; not just ordinary privates in the huge army of the bereaved."[4] So, now the ego has gotten involved and is pushing its way to the forefront: _Look at me! Look how I am suffering!_

Consider the poetry that Jason Towner, recently separated from his wife, wrote after he read Lewis' _A Grief Observed_:

It is as if I have walked from darkness into the light.
I have learned something about myself.
For all these months, I have carried the torch,
motivated by some hidden desire
to show everyone how much I love you,
even after you left.

VANITY. As if I could now prove something
which I never had to prove before.
So what if I am one of the world's greatest lovers
or the most long-suffering, or the most patient . . .

Oh, I've loved you dramatically
And I've held on to you
even after you asked me to let go.
It is as if I am trying to prove to all our friends
how much I loved you.
There was a nagging fear that I thought
that perhaps they thought that
maybe I was not such a good husband, after all,
"Why would she leave him?"

Have I retained you like an old letter jacket?
Have I treated you as a possession?
Something to remind me of days long ago?
We keep things until our attics and closets and
garages and basements are full.
So now I must let go.
 I've won.
All my friends have been impressed by my loyalty to you.
But . . .
They have been saddened by my grief.
They want their friend to be well again.
But . . .
I showed them, didn't I?[6]

Reread Towner's words. Underline the words or phrases with which you can identify.

You may have underlined phrases such as: *I've held on to you even after you asked me to let go; as if I could now prove something; treated you as a possession; they want their friend to be well again.*

Charlotte Elliott, an invalid for most of her life, wrote the words to "Just As I Am" in 1834, after she wrestled with a great sense of helplessness. She had become a Christian after a deep conversation with a Swiss evangelist, Cesar Malan.[7] Her handicap so emotionally shaped Charlotte that she must have wondered at times whether Jesus would want her, invalid though she was. Through her conversion, Charlotte came to Jesus just as she was—handicap and all, and the popular hymn that she wrote reflected that conviction.

Some of us have sung the hymn or heard it sung so many times, we tune out the words, particularly in the third verse: "Just as I am, tho' tossed about/With many a conflict, many a doubt/Fightings within and fears without/O Lamb of God, I come! I come!" *Fightings within and fears without*— That phrase has long captured my curiosity. Could it be referring to those wounds and scars deep within the human spirit? Was the poet suggesting that we come to Jesus with those? Yes, I think so. "Just As I Am" is not just a hymn for the close of a service. It is an invitation for those who have strayed from Jesus to come back to Him with their wounds and their scars.

What prevents you from coming to Jesus, just as you are?

_____

_____

Regardless of what has happened to you . . . you are no martyr, no hero . . . just a human being who hurts.[5]

Divorce is a process, not simply an event for me. I will quit dwelling on my old wounds.

➠ Stop and pray, asking God to help you realize that Jesus accepts you with all your wounds and scars.

Weekly Work

➠ Repeat the affirmation appearing in the margin.

DAY 4

Today's objective:
You will review the path to divorce and to recovery.

Discovering Paths to Recovery

While riding with another driver, have you suddenly realized the driver is going a different way than the path you take? Eventually you ask, "Where are you going?" That happens in a marriage, only in your case, one party had a different destination: divorce. Or while you both realized divorce was occurring, you chose different paths to get there.

Advice on how to divorce "successfully" is readily available. Be around an embittered, angry, divorced individual and prepare not only to get advice but also to get sprayed with venom. That's why the divorced person, particularly the recently divorced person, must be cautious where he/she seeks advice. Not everyone's goal is the high road of recovery. Some keep reminding God that justice is a little overdue where a person's ex is concerned. Some walk in the present constantly glancing back over their shoulders, like Lot's wife, rather than looking expectantly into the future to which God is calling them.

Here are some things to remember as we choose our path:

1. The Lord wants to accompany us on our path.

Reflect on the words of that wonderful spiritual, "Precious Lord, Take My Hand." The song goes, "Precious Lord . . . take my hand. Lead me on, help me stand. I am tired, I am weak, I am worn." Perhaps those words are not strong enough to describe how you feel this moment.

✎ Forgetting poetic rhythm, insert words that capture your feeling.

I am _____.
I am _____.
I am _____.

You may have written something like this: "I am defeated, I am devastated; I am exhausted. I am humiliated." Now, go back and sing that (in your mind, if you prefer) and insert your word choices. (This may be difficult for some people, but the Lord already knows how you feel.) Here are the words to more of the song. I've added some concepts you may be thinking as you read the words. "Through the storm (of divorce), through the night (of loneliness), lead me on to the light/Precious Lord, take my hand . . /lead me on."[8]

I sometimes think that this spiritual should be the "national anthem" of the divorced. But sadly, some of us refuse God's offered hand; many of us pull away. You may not have chosen the path that has led to divorce; someone most likely made that choice for you. But you have a chance, now, to choose the path to recovery. But a word of caution: if you choose recovery, you have to let go of some other choices, like resentment and revenge.

2. Avoid longing for the old paths; they likely aren't an option.

The Book of Exodus tells how Moses led the people out of Egypt. After three days in the desert without water, the same people who were praising now "grumbled against Moses, saying, 'What are we to drink?'" (Exodus 15:24).

Fast forward to chapter 16:2: "In the desert the whole community grumbled against Moses and Aaron." They whined, "If only we had died by the Lord's hand in Egypt! There we sat around pots of meat and ate all the food we wanted, but you have brought us out into this desert to starve this entire assembly to death." (v. 3) What a bunch of whiners! Whiners are still around!

Karen's story

Karen, a recently divorced person, said: "I do not want to get my hopes up. The hole in my heart left by the divorce has not yet started to heal. It's such an awful feeling. Some days I can't bear to face it. I have nightmares frequently. I guess that is all part of the process. I really hate calling it that because it sounds so clinical instead of human. Sometimes this divorce is so consuming, I wish God would just swallow me up and get it over with . . . then I could have some peace."

✎ **Have you ever been in Karen's sneakers? What advice would you offer her?**

_____

I cannot recall reading anywhere in Scripture that Moses kidnapped the Israelites and said: "You're coming out of Egypt with me or else!" Go back and slowly reread Exodus 16:3. Does this whining sound slightly familiar?

✎ **Take a moment and translate the Israelite whine into a more personal whine. I've done an example for you in the margin.**

_____

_____

_____

If only I were still married! I remember our home in Nashville. There we sat around and had fried chicken and pot roast on Sunday and all the coconut cake I wanted . . .

Whining tends to be habitual. Look at Exodus 17:1-3. The Israelites are not only grumbling, they are now quarreling. Even on the edge of the promised land, the Israelites grumbled. "If only we had died in Egypt! Or in this desert!" However, this time they go a step further and snarl, "Wouldn't it be better for us to go back to Egypt?" (Numbers 14:2-3). Sadly, some divorced people would rather marry again (their equivalent of going back to Egypt) than wrestle with the tough issues of recovery.

Apparently, the Israelites had short memories. Not only had they forgotten the misery of Egypt but also the reality their ancestral parents, Adam and Eve, discovered. Read Genesis 3:24 appearing in the margin. After God drove Adam and Eve from Paradise because of their sin, He placed cherubim with a

After he drove the man out, he placed on the east side of the Garden of Eden cherubim and a flaming sword flashing back and forth to guard the way to the tree of life.

–Genesis 3:24

flaming sword at the entrance to the Garden to block any attempts to go back. In some cases, we can't go back to what we once had; it's not a flaming cherubim, but maybe our ex has remarried, so a new reality blocks the path.

3. Paths to divorce and recovery are not identical.

If you lived in Kansas City and want to go to Louisville, you first probably would consult a map. Or you'd talk to a friend who has driven that trip. You have to answer such questions as: How much time does traveling there take? Do you want the scenic route or the most direct route? Sometimes I have rushed from Kansas City to Louisville. I drove with a "just-get-there" mentality. On other occasions I have "lolly-gagged" to Louisville and stopped for a lot of billboard-advertised antique stores.

Divorce is a journey, not a destination. Divorce is not geometry, where the shortest distance between two points is a straight line. Some take that approach in relationship to divorce. So separation to divorce, what's the most convenient path? How quickly can it be done? Or over with? Settled?

Let's look at two systems of paths. One path, adapted from Wayne Oates, one of the leading thinkers of pastoral care in this country, goes this way:
• Husband and wife stop keeping track of each other's whereabouts.
• Spouses stop turning to each other during needy times.
• Spouses stop touching each other or desiring to be around each other.
• They stop having marital relations with each other.
• Husband and wife stop living together.
Finally, they stop being a couple.[9]

Sometimes couples don't experience these steps in this order. For example, some couples stop having sex long before they cease keeping track of each other. Sometimes, the initiator keeps having sex as a way to camouflage his or her plans; this deeply confounds the spouse that is left. Or one agrees to sex to get the initiator to "change" his/her mind. The issue can be clouded because given the size of the residence and work schedules, some couples can be divorced but still live under the same roof.

 In the margin beside the model above, number the steps in the order in which you experienced them in your marriage. Identify the step which has caused you the greatest difficulty.

I now want to shift attention to the divorce path I think is common:

1. Tension: Most marriages have some tensions; some are able to cope with a great deal of tension. Some couples simply resolve to "make the best of it." Tension, if ignored, often leads to the next point—crisis.

2. Crisis: They take positions, dig in like combatants, and draw lines in the sand, so to speak. The crisis erupts, for example, when unfaithfulness is discovered, when a spouse is arrested for drunken driving, or when one spouse's behavior or some choice becomes "the last straw."

3. Decision Level I: One person verbalizes what he/she has been thinking, often in a generic phrase like, "I need some space." In my case, my divorce was launched when my wife called me while I was on an out-of-town-business trip and said, "I rented an apartment today."

4. Upheaval in various degrees of intensity follows. People have the option of making their parting cruel or civil. The more people do to end their marriage in a civil, humane way, the better off everyone will be.

5. Early transition. Survival. "Help me make it through the night/day/week/month . . .." Dazed existence. Some of us get through the early adjustment, an hour at a time, and some hours have more than 60 minutes. We take baby steps. We do things we never dreamed we could do alone. Eventually we look back on these days of early transition as a grown child looks back on the growth marks on a door frame.

6. Decision/Escalation. However long the separation, a moment occurs when one party wants a decision. Sometimes the abandoned spouse who has determined not to oppose a divorce says, "Make up your mind." Others simply want to get on with their lives. They argue, "I can't live in limbo."

Ironically, sometimes the initiator stalls short of the dotted line, "It all seems so final." On the other hand, some people have rushed into a premature relationship. Indeed, four potential decisions exist:
- Decision to divorce.
- Decision to delay the divorce.
- Decision to reconcile and put the marriage back together.
- Decision to escalate the stakes.

By this point, some people have had the "nice guy/gal" edge worn off, and they turn into "balancing the scales." Goaded by lawyers or informal advisers—often themselves divorced—the tension may intensify as both parties battle for best position. Occasionally, not unlike warring factions grabbing for land before a cease fire, some adopt a strategy of "wearing down" their ex, until they finally agree to anything to "just get it over."

7. New Transition. At this point some feel rage, especially if they are engaged in a full-fledged courthouse "shoot out" with the meters of both attorneys running. A few breathe with relief for the first time in a while; others know only pain, agony and exhaustion. The state says officially, "It's over" and gives you a document stating as much. Sometimes, however, your emotions need time to catch up.

8. Decision Level II: You now sit in the center of a four-way intersection; some of us resemble a car that finds itself in the intersection and the driver has just realized that he zoomed through a stop sign; we zoom on. Some perhaps throw the car in reverse. Others stop dead and try to decide: which direction? Do I seek recovery? Do I seek revenge? Do I seek a rebound relationship: sexual? play house? hasty marriage? Do I just "get on with life?"

Choosing the high road

Of course, if putting the marriage back together truly is not an option, I hope you will choose the high road to recovery. I hope you at least will restore civil communication with and extend forgiveness to your ex. However, some of us have post-marital "resumes" of sorts, with a variety of choices, some good/some bad. Sometimes, with all good intent, we take the high road toward recovery, but somewhere en route, we veer off on a tempting side road. Sometimes in our vulnerability, we make poor choices: emotionally, financially, sexually and/or spiritually. However, the good news is that God is the God of the second chance. Jason Towner structured a question, appearing on the next page, that will bring this lesson to a close:

Can I trust God enough
to totally commit all my weight
to believing
He wants the best for me
and that His will for me is the best?[10]

Recovery does not mean that we totally eradicate the presence of the one we once loved—in fact, we may still love, or at least like, our ex. Towner says it like this: "I did not stand at a casket or graveside to say good-bye to Jane. But, our farewell was just as final. I said good-bye to the person and ten months later to the memory. I looked around for a brief moment. Then I turned out the light, pulled the door shut, heard it lock, and slowly walked up the corridor that would lead to my healing. Jane now occupies a quiet place in my heart."[11]

Weekly Work

✎ **In the margin write what this week's memory verse means to you.**

Think again about the following elements of the "path" described on pages 21-22. Can you recall a moment or instance in each one where God took you by the hand? If so describe that instance beside the element below.

TENSION: _____

CRISIS: _____

DECISION LEVEL I: _____

UPHEAVAL: _____

EARLY TRANSITION: _____

DECISION/ESCALATION: _____

NEW TRANSITION: _____

DECISION LEVEL II: _____

⇒ **Repeat the affirmation appearing in the margin.**

Learning Recovery Agendas

Recovery. Webster's Ninth New Collegiate Dictionary has a lot to say about this wonderful word.[12]

✎ **Below check all the definitions that you think apply to the word** *recovery.*
- ❑ A. "to get back"
- ❑ B. "to bring back to normal position or condition"
- ❑ C. "to make up for . . ."
- ❑ D. "to gain by legal process"
- ❑ E. "to find or identify again"
- ❑ F. "to obtain from ore, a waste product or by-product"
- ❑ G. "to save from loss and restore to usefulness"
- ❑ H. "to regain a normal position or condition"
- ❑ I. "to obtain a final legal judgment in one's favor"
- ❑ J. "to get over"

When God took you by the hand

Divorce is a process, not simply an event for me. I will pay attention to the path to recovery.

DAY
5

Today's objective:
You will become familiar with the agendas of divorce recovery.

In the ashes of our dreams of the
perfect marriage, we can find
nutrients for the future.

If you checked all of the definitions except J, then you agree with the people at Merriam-Webster. "To get over" is a definition that is more "pop" than based in fact. I suggest that people do not, in fact, get over a divorce; rather they reconcile themselves to the experience, even when they and their spouse are unable to reconcile the marriage. To launch our discussion I will focus on definition "F": *to obtain from ore, a waste product or a by-product*. In the ashes of our dreams of the perfect marriage, we can find nutrients for the future.

In 1914 scientist Thomas Alva Edison learned that his Edison Electric Company was on fire. Instead of being devastated as he watched the fire, he instructed aides, "Go get Mama (Mrs. Edison). She's never going to see this color of orange again." This inventor's company was burning and all he could focus on was the colors of the fire. "Don't you realize that you'll be a poor man by dawn?" one aide asked. "Everything you own is going up in flames!" "Nonsense," he retorted. "The only thing burning is my mistakes!" The most valuable resources of Thomas A. Edison were housed in his brain, not inside his factory.[13] Indeed, some of the greatest Edison discoveries occurred after the great fire.

Ashes nourish dreams. You are like ore; the intensity of the heat of the divorce will force waste products from you to be abandoned and by-products to be capitalized on. I own a beautiful, multicolored, translucent heart figurine that was blown from ashes from the Mt. St. Helen's volcano. I never would have believed that out of such ugly grayness could come such exquisite beauty.

Beauty out of ashes

That's where some of you are as you read this. *Beauty*, you scoff. *Out of ashes? That will be the day!* Well, consider another example. A stained-glass window in a church or cathedral isn't made out of solid sheets of glass. The glass must be broken, shaped, chipped to fit the master design of the person crafting it. In the eye of a master craftsman, even slivers of glass matter.

A Focus on Decisions

Many people rely on the theory by Elisabeth Kubler-Ross, published in 1969 in *On Death and Dying* and say that people recovering from divorce go through the same five stages as do people who experience grief over the loss of a loved one. Those stages are denial, anger, bargaining, depression, and acceptance.[14] I believe that Kubler-Ross has helped change the way people think about divorce. Instead of looking at stages, however, in this study we will confront the agendas–or decisions–for healing and recovery.

By their fruit you will recognize them . . . Every good tree bears good fruit, but a bad tree bears bad fruit. A good tree cannot bear bad fruit, and a bad tree cannot bear good fruit . . . Thus by their fruit you will recognize them.
                                    –Matthew 7:16-20

A Time for Healing: Coming to Terms with Your Divorce is based on decision-making rather than on feelings or stages. Unless people make the decision to heal, they will not heal. Recovery is a series of decisions. How do you know when your recovery is a reality? In Matthew 7:16-20, Jesus was asked how to recognize believers and false prophets. Look at the Scripture appearing in the margin at left.

What word do you think would symbolize "fruit" when divorce recovery is concerned? I suggest we expand "fruit" to mean, *By their behaviors, decisions, and attitudes you will recognize that they have recovered*. Alan Wolfelt has formulated a wonderful measurement to analyze those who have become reconciled to their grief. I adapted his assessment to come up with the following inventory for recovery from divorce:

✎ **Below check the blank beside each statement you think describes you.**

People who have "recovered" from their divorce should be able to demonstrate—
❑ a recognition of the reality and finality of the divorce;
❑ a return to stable eating and sleeping patterns that existed before divorce;
❑ a renewed sense of energy and personal well-being;
❑ a subjective sense of release or relief from the spouse. (They have thoughts about the person but are not preoccupied with these thoughts);
❑ the capacity to enjoy life experiences that should be enjoyable;
❑ the establishment of new and healthy relationships;
❑ the capacity to live a full life without feelings of false guilt or lack of self-respect;
❑ the capacity to organize and plan your life toward the future;
❑ the capacity to become comfortable with the way things are rather than attempting to make things as they were;
❑ the capacity to be open to more change in your life;
❑ the awareness that you have allowed yourself to fully grieve and have survived the experience;
❑ the awareness that you do not "get over grief" but instead are able to acknowledge, "This is my new reality, and I am ultimately the one who must work to create new meaning and purpose in my life;"
❑ the capacity to acknowledge new parts of yourself that you discovered in the growth through your grief;
❑ the capacity to adjust to the new role changes that have resulted from the loss of the relationship;
❑ the capacity to be compassionate with yourself when normal resurgences of intense grief occur (holidays, anniversaries, birthdays, special occasions);
❑ the capacity to acknowledge that the pain of loss is an inherent part of life that results from the ability to give and receive love.[15]

If you have checked 10 or more of the 16 items listed, consider yourself on the way to recovery. Fewer than 10 checked indicates that you still have room for some serious work.

You may find yourself asking, "Can't I recover on my own? Why do I need a group?" Before we answer that, you might be interested to see why you think you do not need a group setting.

✎ **Describe any fears you have about being in a divorce recovery group.**

_____

_____

The value of others' support

You may have answered something like this: "I don't want other people to see how much I'm hurting. I'm embarrassed to admit in front of others that I made some mistakes in my marriage."

Not only do I believe in the value of small groups, I participate in one, not as a leader. I need to be able to bounce ideas off others, to appreciate their experiences and recovery paths. I wish a divorce-recovery movement had been in place when I went through my divorce in 1975-76. I then drove 30 miles to a certified counselor. I am thankful that I made that decision, but I wish a group within the church had been available as well. I am grateful today that materials such as this one are available for churches to use to help people who hurt.

Agendas for Healing for Divorced People

I have adapted the material I label the "agendas" of divorce recovery from the pioneering work of Therese A. Rando, particularly her research in "complicated mourning" which is the delay or denial of healing due to compromise, distortion or failure to acknowledge the processes of mourning.[16] The following are the agendas we will confront in this study.

1. To fully recognize your divorce as a process rather than an event.
2. To intentionally relinquish attachments to your ex and to other relationships.
3. To revise the old assumptive world of the way things are "supposed to be."
4. To readjust to the new realities in your life.
5. To resist counterfeit/discount relationships.
6. To redeem the process and to accept the invitation to resurrection.
7. To reformulate a realistic understanding of adult sexual expression.
8. To review holiday traditions and celebrations in order to create new celebrations.
9. To understand the biblical perspective on divorce and remarriage.

Scripture and the Business of Agendas

A Bible passage that has long stuck with me—the story of a wrestling match at Bethel—applies to divorce recovery. In Genesis 32, the Bible character Jacob camped out alone, only to be "jumped" by a strong wrestler; the match went on all night with neither able to get a decisive pin. As daylight neared, the wrestler wrenched Jacob's hip. Still Jacob did not loosen his grip. "Let go of me!" the wrestler bellowed. Jacob would not break his grip but offered the wrestler one option: "I will not let you go unless you bless me." (Genesis 32:26). The wrestler responded, "What is your name?" "Jacob," was the reply.

The wrestler promised: "Your name will no longer be Jacob, but Israel. . .." Slowly Jacob loosened his hold, "because you have struggled with God and with men and have overcome." (v. 28) The match was over. Eventually, Jacob, now Israel, limped toward home. All the rest of his life, Israel limped.

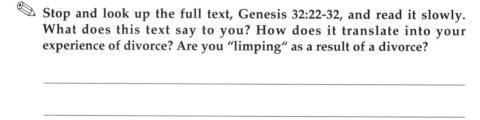 **Stop and look up the full text, Genesis 32:22-32, and read it slowly. What does this text say to you? How does it translate into your experience of divorce? Are you "limping" as a result of a divorce?**

_____

_____

Jacob's experience became real to me in a pastoral counselor's office late one afternoon in 1975. I was all cried out; a stack of used tissues littered the office floor. My kind counselor, Hugh Eichelberger, reminded me of this passage and suggested, "Don't let go of this thing called divorce until it blesses you." *Blesses me? What an insane misuse of Scripture,* I thought. Now, years later, I look back and see the wisdom and tenderness of his suggestion.

Sadly, some of us not only will wrestle our exes and their lawyers but also "the other party" who helped upend our world, with children, in-laws, and well-meaning but silent friends who "just don't know what to say to us . . .." We will take on God, too—because we think God has not come through for us.

Obtaining a blessing

Some of these agendas will lock you in a "submission hold." They will challenge you to think, to feel, but ultimately to make a good decision that will move you closer to reality. You can obtain blessing only through wrestling with the process.

Weekly Work

 Meditate on this week's memory verse. As a result of studying this segment, what does this verse now say to you?

_____

Divorce is a process, not simply an event for me. I may walk with a limp, but I will limp toward recovery.

⮞ **Repeat the affirmation appearing at left.**

_____

Notes

[1] Oscar Handlin and Lillian Handlin, *A Restless People: Americans in Rebellion, 1770-1787.* Garden City, Doubleday, 1982, 90.

[2] Kevin McCarthy, *The On Purpose Person* (Colorado Springs: Navpress, 1992), 96.

[3] Ibid.

[4] C. S. Lewis, *A Grief Observed* (New York: Bantam, 1961), 70.

[5] Taken from the book, *Jason Loves Jane (But They Got a Divorce)* by Jason Towner. Copyright ©1978 by Impact Books, a division of Benson Co. Used by permission of Zondervan Publishing House.

[6] Ibid., 164-165.

[7] William J. Reynolds, *Songs of Glory: Stories of 300 Great Hymns and Gospel Songs* (Grand Rapids: Zondervan, 1990), 162.

[8] Thomas A. Dorsey, "Precious Lord, Take My Hand," Copyright ©1938 by Unichappell Music, Inc. Copyright renewed. International copyright secured. All rights reserved.

[9] Adapted from the work of Wayne E. Oates. *Pastoral Care and Counseling in Grief and Separation.* (Philadelphia: Fortress, 1976), 24-28.

[10] Towner, 169.

[11] Ibid.

[12] *Webster's Ninth New Collegiate Dictionary* (Springfield, MA: Merriam-Webster, 1983), 985.

[13] Material derived from James D. Newton. *Uncommon Friends.* San Diego: Harcourt Brace and Jovanovich, 1987, 16, as well as from the author's three-hour conversation with James Newton in 1988.

[14] Elisabeth Kubler-Ross, *On Death and Dying* (New York: Macmillian, 1969)

[15] Alan Wolfelt, *Death and Grief: A Guide for Clergy* (Muncie, Indiana: Accelerated Development, 1988), 63.

[16] Adapted from the work of Therese A. Rando. "The Increasing Prevalence of Complicated Mourning: The Onslaught Is Just Beginning," *OMEGA—Journal of Death and Dying,* Vol. 26(1), (1992-93): 43-59.

Relinquishing Attachments

This week's agenda:
You will intentionally relinquish some attachments to your ex and to other relationships.

DETERMINED TO SELF-DESTRUCT

Elizabeth told this story: "When Emma arrived, she didn't want to sit down. She said she'd just stand in front of the fireplace.

"'Elizabeth', she said, 'I've kept quiet as long as I'm going to. I know the loss of Greg has been devastating. That's why over the past few months, when I saw you being so self-destructive, I never criticized . . . . But I have lost my patience. . . . I want you to know that I really am angry at you . . . . You are acting as if you want to lose everything in your life, not just your husband. You seem to think that alone, you are nothing.

"'But, there's something very important I think you've forgotten,' Emma went on to say. 'You were a whole person before you met Greg, and you can be a whole person after him. . . . We have been best friends for a long time, but I won't have your craziness in my life anymore . . . . If you want to stop trying to destroy your life and start being the terrific person you really are, then I'm your friend forever. But if you don't, then don't count me in on anything you are doing.'"[1]

What could Emma see that Elizabeth needed in her life? Read about this on page 33.

What you'll learn

This week you will—
- recollect memories and impressions from marriage;
- examine the actions, attitudes, and ambivalences of you and your ex;
- define the elements that remain knotted;
- relinquish old attachments to the ex;
- loosen old attachments to the relationships linked to your marriage.

What you'll study

Memories and Impressions	Examining the Triple A's	Defining the Knotted Elements	Actively Relinquishing Attachments	Loosening the Old Attachments
DAY 1	DAY 2	DAY 3	DAY 4	DAY 5

Memory verses

This week's verses of Scripture to memorize—

But one thing I do: forgetting what is behind and straining toward what is ahead, I press on toward the goal to win the prize for which God has called me heavenward in Christ Jesus.

—Philippians 3:13-14

Memories and Impressions

Today's objective:
You will recollect memories and impressions from the marriage.

Webster's Ninth New Collegiate Dictionary defines *to recollect* as *to bring back to the level of conscious awareness.*[2] The term is based on French and Latin words which mean "to gather again." To remember realistically and accurately—to gather again— is an important agenda item. Just as people may have selective hearing—they hear what they want to hear—so we may have selective memory. Here are some things we will learn in divorce recovery about memories:

1. Memories must be treasured. We learn the importance of actively and not just passively remembering our grief. A friend truly can assist a divorced person by helping him or her remember completely and clearly and then allowing that person to forget. Sometimes in groups someone will preface a statement by saying, "I hadn't thought of this in years!"

2. Memories must be disciplined. Memories can dart in and make total havoc of our emotions. Some memories just show up unannounced. Undisciplined memories sabotage some "baby steps" in our recovery.

3. Memories must be interpreted. I recall my ex insisting that we really needed to be saving money. We were trying to pay off graduate-school loans, thinking about having a child, and wanting to buy a home. So, her suggestion seemed logical. However, after she left, the memory hit me. I could hear her saying, "We really do need to be saving money." I thought: *She wanted to save money so she could take that money and leave.* Look at the memory path below.

Grieving is a curious process of forgetting, remembering, and forgetting again. The ultimate goal of grief work is to be able to remember without pain.[3]

In the early days of our divorce, we often sift for any shred of evidence indicating premeditated decision-making. In this instance, the longer I thought about it, the more angry I became. This interpretation convinced me that for a long time she had been planning to leave. *Save money! Sure. Now I understood.* Eventually, I confronted her with my interpretation. No, she explained, she had not suggested that we save money so she would have a nest egg for a new life without me. Jane explained that her family members always had been savers; she merely was reflecting that family commitment.

I apologized for jumping to conclusions—although the act of apologizing in that instance did not prevent me from future misinterpretations. I struggled many times with her explanations, but my track record of jumping to conclusions—often the wrong conclusion—convinced me that she was right.

▶ Go through your memory videos and select a memory that annoys or taunts you. Press "play." Slowly let it run across your screen. Is it possible . . . just possible . . . that like me, you have misinterpreted memories big time and thus have empowered them to hurt you? Ask God to help you reassess your interpretations and to show you if you have misinterpreted the dream. When/if we are anxious to be right and for our exes to be wrong, we set ourselves up to misinterpret.

✎ **Below write out the essence of a troublesome interpreted memory.**

The situation: _____

What your ex said/did: _____

What you said/did: _____

Take a moment to review the memory and the interpretation you have assigned it. Continue:

The possibility now occurs to me that _____

_____

What can you do with this "fresh" insight? _____

_____

When I admitted my immature behaviors and confessed, healing began.

4. Memories get our attention. Sometimes, we are so locked in to making ourselves look good/making the ex look bad that we focus on what he or she did and tiptoe over some of our own inadequacies, mild outrages, and failures as a spouse. After my divorce I kept saying, "But she left me." Fact: Jane did move out and initiated the divorce action. However, many times I winced as I remembered something I had done and said which hurt Jane. Through these vignettes God began to deal with the festering but submerged issues in my life that needed attention. When I resisted owning up, the same short videos of memories rewound and replayed, sometimes with even more intensity. But when I admitted my immature behaviors and confessed, healing began.

5. Some memories are sex-based. Many divorced people used fighting as a prelude to sex; sex was a way to "kiss and make up" without having to formally say, "I'm sorry" or to work on issues. Sometimes, a song, a sound, or something out of the clear blue sky causes a sexual memory from the marriage to play on the big screen. Trying to dodge memories by yelling the mental equivalent of "Scat!" is like trying not to think of hot-fudge sundaes. Try putting hot-fudge sundaes out of your mind, and you hardly can keep from throwing down this book and dashing to the nearest snack shop and screaming, "Hot-fudge sundae!"

Eventually, as these memories occurred, I realized that my soul really was missing the sexual intimacy of my marriage. I sometimes had to say, "Lord, I can do nothing about this memory. I do miss this wonderful gift you gave. Help me to realize that perhaps someday regular sexual intimacy in marriage again will be part of my life. But don't let me settle for the discounts today."

This is . . . how we set our hearts at rest in his presence whenever our hearts (or memories) condemn us. For God is greater than our hearts (or memories) and he knows everything.

–1 John 3:19-20

6. Memories may help us set agendas for counseling. Memories may keep knocking at our emotional doors and may prompt us to seek counseling to explore a memory and its deeper meaning. Maybe God wants you to go to a skilled counselor to work through the memory. Some memories have to be defused, almost like a bomb. Look in the margin and consider these comforting words from John. The first time through, skip over the words in the parentheses; the second time substitute the parenthesized words and give it some inflection in your voice.

> Regardless of how this memory feels, it does not have to harm me. I will look for the kernel of blessing in the memory as I relinquish my attachment to memories of my ex and my marriage.

DAY 2

Today's objective:
You will examine the actions, attitudes, and ambivalences of you and your ex.

A divorce postmortem

 Pause for prayer. Talk to God about what specifically troubles you with a particular memory.

Weekly Work

✎ Begin to memorize this week's memory verses, Philippians 3:13-14. Write them three times in the margin.

 Say aloud the affirmation appearing at left.

Examining the Triple A's

The philosopher Plato declared that the unexamined life is not worth living. I would add that the unexamined divorce will not lead to recovery. As I grew up, I always was quick to turn "state's evidence" against my brother or sister. Sometimes during a conflict, my dad asked, "And what is your side of the story?" He knew that in most instances, two points of view existed.

So it is with divorce. We live in a society that has made blaming others something of an art form. Yet we need to ask five questions:
1. What happened?
2. When did it happen?
3. Who caused it to happen?
4. Why did it happen?
5. How can we keep this from happening again or to another person?

✎ **Answer these questions about your divorce. Instead of trying to do this here, use extra paper. Your answers may be lengthy.**

    1. What happened?
    2. When did it happen?
    3. Who caused it?
    4. Why did it happen?
    5. How could another divorce be avoided?

However you answered questions 1 through 4, I hope you said that "working on recovery" was a way to avoid another divorce. People in the medical world conduct autopsies or postmortems as a way to learn what happened or what went wrong. The purpose of our study today is to do just that—to examine actions, attitudes, and ambivalences during/after a divorce.

1. Actions. Some couples have long histories of verbal duels; many have the scars as proof. Sadly, many of these duels have not been "behind closed doors" but have been quite public. We commonly focus on what the ex or initiator did, particularly if we are getting good reviews in the role of victim. Sometimes we recall not just the sins of commission (what I or he/she did) but also sins of omission (what I or she/he did not do).

Remember how (before the days of the photocopier) we used file cards to conduct research for writing term papers? We would amass a stack of file cards for our notes and then place them in the little green metal box. I maintain that we are still file-card keepers. We note every injustice, slight, and marital wrong, and dutifully record it on the file card for future reference: "I saw that!" and we immediately fill out a file card: date, time, offense.

✎ On the file cards in the margin write out actions/attitudes that you still consider offensive by your ex.

Some items on the file cards are grave, others are borderline ridiculous. They may make sense to the grieved party. Towner wrote, "Petty things killed our marriage. They were the silent bullets which killed."[4] It's not the big things but the slow gradual accumulation that often causes difficulties. Little things build up, and many adults demand compound interest. We often feel tempted to reach for another file card. We need to discard file cards and not just make room for new ones with the latest offenses.

Gigy and Kelly administered to 437 men and women divorcing in the mid-1980s the following 28-item checklist on reasons for divorce. *The Journal of Divorce and Remarriage* published the results.

✎ Check all of the following that were/are important factors in the breakdown of your marriage and decision to divorce.

❑ 1. Gradual growing apart, losing sense of closeness
❑ 2. Not feeling loved and appreciated by spouse
❑ 3. Sexual intimacy problems
❑ 4. Serious difference in lifestyle or values
❑ 5. Spouse not able/willing to meet my major needs
❑ 6. Frequently felt put down or belittled by spouse
❑ 7. Emotional problems of spouse
❑ 8. Conflict regarding spending and dealing with money
❑ 9. Severe and intense conflict, frequent fighting
❑ 10. Problems and conflicts with roles, i.e., division of responsibility for household jobs or other chores outside of the house
❑ 11. Employment or job-related difficulties
❑ 12. Spouse angry, demanding
❑ 13. Spouse's jealousy of you and/or your activities
❑ 14. Boredom with spouse and/or marriage
❑ 15. Conflict regarding child rearing, discipline
❑ 16. Spouse not reliable.
❑ 17. Career conflicts between you and spouse
❑ 18. Serious financial problems
❑ 19. Extramarital affair(s) of spouse
❑ 20. Spouse's alcohol abuse
❑ 21. Other: (specify) _____
❑ 22. Your own extramarital affair(s)
❑ 23. Violence between you and spouse
❑ 24. Spouse too dependent on or closely tied to own family
❑ 25. Spouse's drug abuse
❑ 26. Own alcohol abuse
❑ 27. Severe or chronic illness
❑ 28. Own drug abuse[5]

Go back to the list. In the margin to the left of the box, number from 1 to 10, with 10 being the most serious and 1 the least serious, the problems in order of their severity in your marriage. How well did you match up with the 189 males and 212 females who participated in this study? (See the survey outcome on page 43.) You might be intrigued to know that those self-reported reasons changed across the years, as people either became adjusted to the divorce, intensified their denial of the real reasons for the divorce, or arrived at such a point of healing that they could be more realistic.

2. Attitudes. We commonly explain improper behavior by saying, "He/she just has a bad attitude!" Sometimes we need friends lovingly to remind us, "Watch your attitude."

Elizabeth told this story: "When Emma arrived, she didn't want to sit down. She said she'd just stand in front of the fireplace.

Elizabeth's story

"'Elizabeth', she said, 'I've kept quiet as long as I'm going to. I know the loss of Greg has been devastating. That's why over the past few months, when I saw you being so self-destructive, I never criticized . . .. But I have lost my patience . . . . I want you to know that I really am angry at you . . . . You are acting as if you want to lose everything in your life, not just your husband. You seem to think that alone, you are nothing.

"'But, there's something very important I think you've forgotten,' Emma went on to say. 'You were a whole person before you met Greg, and you can be a whole person after him . . .. We have been best friends for a long time, but I won't have your craziness in my life anymore . . .. If you want to stop trying to destroy your life and start being the terrific person you really are, then I'm your friend forever. But if you don't, then don't count me in on anything you are doing.'"[6]

✎ **Emma did her friend Elizabeth a big favor when she confronted her. Who has Emma-ized you? What was the motivation? What has been the outcome of that experience?**

Who? When? _____

How did this person confront? _____

What was the person's motivation? _____

What was your initial reaction? _____

What is your relationship today? _____

What part has this played in your recovery or desire for recovery? _____

_____

▥▶ **Stop and pray, thanking God for this experience of confrontation. If the relationship with the person confronting you still is strained, ask God if you need to make a move toward healing. Think about one thing you could do in the next 24 hours to begin to mend the distance.**

3. Ambivalences. We are such a logic-oriented society, we believe that if we just keep at it, we eventually can solve the lingering puzzle surrounding our divorce. Sometimes, the initiator can't verbalize all of the reasons for leaving. Sometimes "I need space" or "I need my own place" doesn't reveal that the

ambivalence—having conflicting emotions at the same time: I love and I hate him/her.

initiator already has spent a lot of time and energy reaching this decision. Sometimes the truth involves more than we know although not always more than some of our neighbors or co-workers know. "I was the last to find out," sobbed Marilyn. "I felt like a fool." We may have either innocently or directly ignored the scattered pieces of evidence. Silences. Not initiating sex. Little inconsistencies in stories about working late. However, some divorce stories never will make sense, and we must live with the mystery.

Sometimes, ambivalences occur; you may not tell some things because you have children. For example, many like Cynthia have discovered that a husband is not in love with another woman but another man; husbands have discovered the "other" is a woman. Cynthia did not tell her children or her pastor, since she reasoned, "He's still their father." She took enormous heat for her explanation, "I just don't love him anymore," which sidestepped the actual reason for the divorce. Sometimes someone does not or cannot disclose crucial bits of data. One woman's husband told her, "Go ahead and tell, but if I lose my job, how will I make child-support payments?"

When we determine that we cannot love or contribute without marriage, we work against ourselves.

The process of relinquishing our attachments to our ex will not be easy. The process is complicated because it is branded with the word "failure." When we determine that we cannot love or contribute without marriage, we close ourselves off from receiving good things. We gaze into the reflecting pool of life and muddy the waters, for we have decided what we must see before we even look.

Weekly Work

➡ **Continue to memorize this week's memory verses. Think about what new meaning you find in this passage because of your writing, listening, sharing, and reflecting in this unit.**

DAY 3

Today's objective:
You will define the elements that remain knotted in your relationship with your ex.

Defining the Knotted Elements

One unrecognized aspect of divorce is that it changes the relationship from spouse to ex—and ex is a real relationship, particularly when children are involved. Today we will study these areas in which relationships change:

1. Children. Children complicate the defining process. We must resolve issues such as: With whom will the children live? How will we finance their needs? Will the children become pawns? I have not talked to my ex in probably 10 years—no real need to talk to her. However, if we had children, I could not ignore talking with her. Sadly, some exes can only talk to each other now through their attorneys.

Every so often parents, in advancing their own agenda and protecting their boundaries from intrusion by their ex, fail to understand the lingering, on-going implications to their children. Sadly, children can become the "footballs" in a rough-and-tumble, no-holds-barred game between parents.

✎ **Review the list on the next page of games single parents play. Mark the ones in which you or someone you know have participated.**

Name the game—

_____

_____

Its characteristic—

_____

_____

_____

- "I spy"—Children become undercover agents and bear intelligence tidbits that may be used for one parent's advantage.
- "Relay"—Children pass on information the parent would rather not pass on. "Oh, by the way, Daddy said to tell you . . . ."
- "Look what he/she made me do!"—blaming the ex for your personal failings.
- "Santa Claus"—"Look what Daddy/Mommy got me for Christmas."
- "Plant the poison"—Repeatedly put down your ex in front of the children.
- Other—Maybe you know of a game not in this list. In the margin box name the game and identify its main characteristic.

Some children pit one parent against the other. Some of their games are: "It's all your fault that I am unhappy! Daddy lets me do this when I'm at his house! I know about X, Y or Z and if you make me mad, I'll tell." You also may be involved in two arenas: with your children and ex and with the children and ex of the person you are dating. Children may have a strong commitment to the "they'll-get-back-together-again" fantasy. If they perceive you as a threat to their fantasy's fulfillment, look out.

2. Property. In some divorce decrees, one parent is allowed to live in the house with the children until the children reach age 18. Then the house must be sold and the money divided. What if your ex does not maintain house or property, so that its eventual sale value is reduced? Finances may be short, so that the spouse defers maintenance.

You may grieve over the loss of a place. How do you feel when you pull up in the driveway and wait in the car for your kids to come out of a home where you once lived? Such moments are great times to invite God to help you.

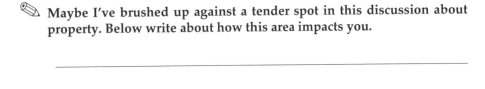 **Maybe I've brushed up against a tender spot in this discussion about property. Below write about how this area impacts you.**

_____

_____

Tough on friends

3. Neighbors. Your divorce can be difficult on your neighbors and friends. If divorce "struck" 404 East 81st Street, couldn't divorce happen at 412 East 81st?

Moreover, a neighbor couple may not be equally attracted to both of you. So, a divorce may mean the loss of one or both of them. If you are good friends as well as neighbors, you may keep in touch, but busyness and change may negate your intentions. Sometimes, especially with custody battles, neighbors get involved in the process. What happens if a car is parked in the driveway at 10:30, 11:30, 12:30 p.m.? What if it is still there at 9:00 a.m. for everyone to see? Neighbors notice things and sometimes pass on their interpretations.

*Neighbor/friend
Friend/ex-neighbor
or ex-neighbor/
ex-friend*

Give your neighbors every chance to understand the divorce. But realize that sometimes they won't understand, or they will prefer to believe the spin your ex puts on the circumstance. You may encounter awkward moments—when you run into former neighbors in the mall and get one of those 90-second, "Hi, how are you? Fine. And you?" conversations. The reality is that you may also have to mourn the loss of neighbors in the divorce process.

Think back to the time of your divorce. Did you lose neighbor(s) in the process? Why do you think the loss occurred? Take a moment and write about that loss. If you had a chance to talk candidly with them today, what would you say?

_____

_____

Perhaps they were indifferent to you, or they took your spouse's side. Or maybe they didn't want to "get involved." Maybe you cut them out of your life. One way you could approach them would be to say, "I felt hurt when you no longer seemed to want to be around me. I would like to sit down and talk with you and tell you how much your friendship meant to me over the years."

4. The church. Divorce can impact faith and your particular faith community. At a point when we most need the church, we feel distanced from it.

Bill tells this story: "'After Patti moved out, I kept going to church. I assumed the word would get out. Then one day after the service, I stopped to shake hands with the pastor, and he said, 'Where's your wife? Is she sick today?' I realized he didn't know. So, I kinda fidgeted and looked down and finally mumbled, 'She, ah . . . she left me.' He said, 'Oh. I'm sorry to hear that.' A lot of people were waiting to shake his hand, and I just turned and walked out the door. I just wanted him to say more than 'Oh. I'm sorry to hear that.'"

 Quickly scan Bill's story. Underline any common elements you share with Bill.

Faith communities react differently to individuals going through a divorce. Some people may be physically thrown out of a church over a divorce. Other people may have felt emotionally "thrown out" or "lost" in a predominately couples setting. Some churches have ways, often through silence, of saying, "You no longer are welcome here." Many local churches react to single-adult ministry by saying, "We don't want them here." Obviously, this church where you are participating in this group is a healthy exception.

You may have switched churches because you couldn't go back to the church you and a spouse attended: too many memories. You may have switched churches simply because you felt ignored or ostracized or distanced. The issue of children is a tough reality with some single parents if the custodial parent is not committed to taking them to church or lives a lifestyle contradictory to the church's teachings. If you are the custodial parent, what about weekends the children are with your ex? Will he/she take them to church or see that they are in church? What happens when children miss the steady regularity of a loving Sunday School teacher who knows them by name? For the good of the children you may decide to remain in the church and live with the awkwardness you feel. Large churches may have multiple worship services and Sunday Schools, so you may attend and never see the ex. You also can end up in the same single-adult ministry.

One more loss

Sometimes we have to mourn the loss of a church home, and that becomes one more in our list of losses. Sometimes we need time to let feelings settle; you may need to take a sabbatical from a particular church (I am not advising that you quit going to church). In a few months, you may find that some of the feelings have died down. Sometimes special programs, musical programs, or sports events, will occur in the church, and a child will want you to attend. Talk to the child, talk to your ex, and work out a reasonable response.

 Some divorced people have a stack of file cards focused on their church. Just as you wrote to your neighbors, take a moment to reflect on what you would want to say to your church family.

_____

_____

Many ways exist to keep us "knotted" to our exes, particularly through children. These realities require imagination, creativity, and sensitivity to find working "solutions."

Weekly Work

 Continue to memorize this week's memory verse. How does this verse relate to the task of defining the elements that remain knotted?

▷ **Say aloud the affirmation appearing at left.**

Regardless of how tangled the knot, I will look for positive links with the past.

DAY

4

Today's objective:
I will examine the areas in which I have relinquished attachments and areas in which I need to relinquish attachments to my ex and to the marriage.

Actively Relinquishing Attachments

Some people have difficulty facing reality. They say, "He'll come to his senses if I just give him time," or "She can't really go through with this." When I first was separated, I left the front porch light on, just in case. But finally the night occurred when I walked past the light switch, ignored it, and went to bed.

The word _relinquish_ means _to leave behind_. Another definition is "to stop holding physically."[7] Relinquishing is difficult. "If I let go of him, who am I?" one woman asked.

King David was married to King Saul's daughter Michal. In David's absence, King Saul married Michal to Paltiel. Years passed. When Saul was killed, David became king. By this time David had six wives, but he wanted Michal back. Jewish law forbade a woman going back to her husband if she had married another (Deuteronomy 24:1-4). The story complicates when an ex-Saul aide, Abner, wants to join the inner circle of the new king. David says OK to Abner on one condition: "Give me my wife, Michal" (2 Samuel 3:14).

Scripture reports a glimpse of Paltiel's grief when his wife was taken away and given back to King David. "Her husband, however, went with her, weeping behind her all the way to Bahurim" (v. 16). Can you feel Paltiel's pain? Crying, sobbing, wailing, shrieking: "This can't be happening! She's my wife!" Then at Bahurim, Abner had enough. "Go back home!" he ordered. Paltiel left. This is the last we hear from the brokenhearted man. "Paltiel," noted Ganse Little, "is at least allowed the privilege of a futile protest."[8] Read those words again: _the privilege of a futile protest_. Can you identify with that phrase?

A biblical glimpse at relinquishment

Many of us can, in a day of no-fault divorce, when a divorce can be granted without anyone caring what the non-filing spouse thinks or wants.

Some of us have offered our futile protests. I believe in doing everything within reason to try to stop a divorce process. Years after my divorce, someone asked me, "Can you say that you did everything possible to save your marriage?" I thought a moment, recalled my futile protests—my Paltiel moments—and answered, "Yes, I did."

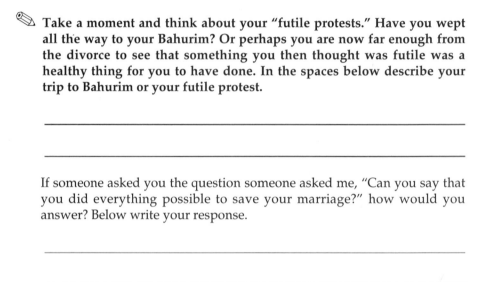 **Take a moment and think about your "futile protests." Have you wept all the way to your Bahurim? Or perhaps you are now far enough from the divorce to see that something you then thought was futile was a healthy thing for you to have done. In the spaces below describe your trip to Bahurim or your futile protest.**

_____

_____

If someone asked you the question someone asked me, "Can you say that you did everything possible to save your marriage?" how would you answer? Below write your response.

_____

_____

If you believe that you took every step humanly possible to keep your marriage from ending, then the remainder of this *A Time for Healing: Coming to Terms of Your Divorce* workbook will help you cope with your divorce in an emotionally healthy way and with God's help will help direct your future. However, if in studying this material God has impressed upon you that hardness of your heart or an unforgiving spirit have kept you from working diligently enough at reconciliation to put your marriage back together, then I encourage you to stop at this point in your pilgrimage and seek help in making another effort at saving your marriage. A book, *Insuring Marriage: 25 Proven Ways to Prevent Divorce* (LifeWay Press, 1994), can help you and your estranged spouse or ex, depending on where you are in the process, take a fresh look at some of these issues together. You can ask your pastor or counselor for help in this matter.

In the story about Michal and King David, merely turning on the road and starting toward home was not the end of Paltiel's relinquishing. That too, like a divorce, is a process. Maybe he lay in the darkness berating himself and saying, "I should have done . . ." What does Paltiel's story say to us?

1. Relinquishing is gradual. Some people carry "the torch" for a long time. Others decide to eliminate all traces of an ex in their lives and in their histories. Ask them about a divorce, and they may snarl or snap, "I don't want to talk about it." A more reasoned approach is to give the relinquishing process time and cooperation. Let the memories gradually fade.

2. Relinquishing may be symbolic. Did you fight over household goods? Who won? Sometimes we infuse a physical object with more meaning than it had during the marriage. Divorcing couples fight over the silliest objects—in one case I know, a gallon pickle jar of nuts, bolts and screws. Where is the object now? Has it retained its value to you? Would you consider returning it to your ex? Perhaps you're locked in the battle now. Ask yourself: Why am I attaching so much meaning to this particular object?

3. Relinquishing may be evoked by very painful moments, such as the remarriage of your ex. Maybe you entertained little fantasies of the two of you getting back together. For a long time after Patti Roberts' very public divorce from Richard Roberts, she remained in Tulsa, where they had lived. She thought she should stay in Tulsa until she was certain that no possibility of reconciliation existed for her and Richard.[9] However, Patti told me that a point arrived when God was nudging her—preparing her for a reality check. That occurred when Tulsa papers announced Richard's remarriage. In the margin box describe at what point you relinquished your ex.

As we will see in a later Agenda, the marriage of the ex becomes a closed door, or as one divorced person has phrased it, a nailed-shut door. Now you also may have to grieve for your lost fantasies of a joyous reconciliation.

4. Relinquishment opens the door to what God wants to do now or next in your life. That day in court I had to relinquish my last fantasy. I kept thinking, even to 24 hours before the court appearance, that somehow the miracle would arrive. Now, I look back and realize I wanted God to perform as I directed. In the session before the court date, my counselor asked, "What are you going to do if God doesn't come through by Friday?" "Not to worry, sir, He'll come through!" I declared confidently. Consider these words in the margin from Jason Towner.

How do you respond to the words of this poem? In my case, perhaps as in yours, no stay of execution happened; on the surface, at least initially, no miracle occurred. The judge signed the papers, tapped his gavel, and my marriage was history.

We do not know how long it took Paltiel to relinquish Michal, if ever. I think it took a long time for Michal to relinquish Paltiel. Scripture offers a couple of slices of evidence. As King David, with 30,000 of his men, returned the Ark, the most sacred of objects to a Jew, to Jerusalem, the city erupted "with rejoicing" (2 Samuel 6:12).

Scripture notes that Michal was not in the crowd, let alone at the king's side. "Michal, daughter of Saul, watched from a window." One translation I read used "watched from a distance." While all Israel celebrated, Michal boycotted the festivities. Moreover, when she saw David leading the party, "she despised him in her heart" (v. 16). The last word of Michal is a simple sentence, packed with commentary on the sex life of the couple, "and Michal daughter of Saul had no children to the day of her death" (v. 23). One scholar noted, "In view of their quarrel we may assume that her former love for David had been wholly transformed to Paltiel and that she never forgave David for taking her away from her husband."[11]

Sometimes, control issues that never were settled during marriage become the battlefields for continued skirmishes after the divorce. For example, do you attempt to control your ex and perhaps your children through the timing of your alimony and/or child-support payments?

I relinquished
when I—

_____

_____

_____

_____

There has to be material to make a fire,
and the potter must have clay to turn his wheel;
there has to be a match to light a candle.
Although He wanted to give a miracle,
the material through which He could work was not available.

What I must remember is that it hurt Him as much as it hurt me that there was no miracle.

So He did what He could with what He had
and it was not second best.
He gave me the peace of forgiveness and moments of joy
and the promise of the future.[10]

✎ **Below write ways you attempt to control your ex—ways which prove that you have some things to learn about relinquishing.**

Schedules: _____

Relationships: _____

Emotions: _____

Money: _____

Other: _____

✎ **It's relinquishment review time. Complete the statements in the margin box. In the first part of the box, describe what you have relinquished so far. In the second part of the box, describe what you have not relinquished.**

➧ **Stop and pray, saying these words:**

Lord, as a result of this lesson, I want to thank you that I have relinquished . . . (name them).
Lord, as a result of this lesson, I realize that I need to relinquish . . . (name them).
Lord, as a result of this lesson, I realize that I need to relinquish some things but I just cannot do so right now. Help me to become willing to relinquish . . . (name them).
Lord, thank you for being interested in my healing. Amen.

Weekly Work

➧ **Say aloud the affirmation appearing in the margin.**

➧ **Take a moment and pray for members of your group. This material today may have been difficult for some of them. Call out the name of each member of your group and ask God to help each person as he or she deals with this material.**

Margin box

What I have relinquished—

_____

_____

_____

_____

What I have not relinquished—

_____

_____

_____

_____

Regardless of how much I enjoy clinging to the past, I am the one who decides when tomorrow begins.

DAY 5

Today's objective:
I will loosen old attachments to the relationships and friendships linked to my former marriage.

Loosening the Old Attachments

Confronting the realities of transition in relationships is another step that faces you. Here are some of those realities.

1. Go through separation/divorce—and eventually future relationships—and you will discover who your real friends are. In fact, going through divorce resembles an airline "milk-run," with many stops and with your friends as passengers. Some will get off at separation, some at divorce, and others at remarriage. Why is divorce so difficult on friends? First, your friends, particularly those who have unhappy marriages, struggle with the thought, "If it happened to them, it could happen to us."

2. Your friends will try to make sense with the pieces of the puzzle they have. They will look for clues to make sense of what is happening. To make the pieces fit they may come to outrageous assumptions: he's/she's met someone—and assumptions may spread like wildfire in the form of gossip.

Paradoxically, good can come from your divorce's impact on friends. Seeing your trauma close up may dispel any budding longings for divorce. You may succeed in making divorce a harsh reality for them rather than an abstract, potentially attractive option.

On the other hand, your presence may make them feel uncomfortable. Or they may be comfortable with you one-on-one or two-on-one, but in a larger setting, particularly a religious group, they may worry that some group members are annoyed by their perceived support of you. Your solo presence may color the event, even among good friends.

3. Social invitations stop or change. Your friends may renege on social invitations you extend or expect. They simply may stop calling. Mutual friends may invite your ex but not you. Your friends may alter the social pattern, so that now just the men or just the women go to dinner. You and your ex may show up at the same social function. This may put a damper on the event.

4. Some friends will work/may have worked to get the two of you back together. Some friends may share your confidences, take sides, or swap details or even hunches with others.

What did your friends do?

A reality among some friends that has forever damaged the friendship is the sexual "come on." A friend of the opposite sex may admit to you that his or her marriage is "no picnic." Some may even express having feelings of attraction to you. In addition to all your problems, now you have this!

Linda told this story: "I had casually said to my friend that I was having some problems with a leaking hose into the washing machine. She said she would have her husband Fred look at it. I thought this was great since I just didn't have the money to call a plumber.

Linda's story

"So one night, Fred dropped by. I showed him the problem and then excused myself when the phone rang. After a little while he called me down to the basement. He told me that he would have to get some materials but would come back Friday night. Then he said, 'How are you doing?' I didn't answer, and he added, 'You know . . . an attractive woman like you must have needs.' Then it dawned on me: my friend's husband was coming on to me in my basement, of all places, with stacks of dirty clothes everywhere and a faucet going drip! drip! drip!"

✎ **What should Linda have done? Circle the most appropriate response.**
   A. Asked him to clarify what he was saying.
   B. Asked him to leave immediately.
   C. Acted as if she didn't know what he was talking about.
   D. Invited him and his wife to dinner so that the wife would be present while he did the repair work.
   E. Called a plumber and fork out the dough.
   F. Told the amorous plumber's wife what had happened.
   G. Ignored it since he possibly was embarrassed afterwards.

It happens! It happens with the "best of friends"—friends who are supposed to understand but who also know, or assume they know, our vulnerability.

6. You'll lose some friends. In many instances, saying good-bye to our friends will be a gradual loss rather than a swift amputation. You suddenly may discover that six months has passed and you haven't heard from a friend. Sometimes it will not make sense to you.

7. Be cautious in judging their intentions and reactions. Fear and social insecurity may cause friends to do strange and yet insensitive things—things they eventually will regret but may be too embarrassed to attempt to rectify.

8. Remember that for every friend you lose in a divorce, eventually you will make a new one—perhaps a stronger friend. Some of us may have been lazy in friendship formation and discover that many of "our" friends were, in fact, our ex's friends. In some relationships, we may have jettisoned some friends because a spouse disapproved. Now may be a time to resurrect that friendship. In the margin box list friends that you consider "lost" because of the divorce, and then list new friends you have made.

9. Let your friends know concrete ways they can help you. Tell them your specific needs. If you decline a social invitation, add the hope for "next time."

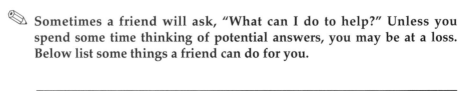 **Sometimes a friend will ask, "What can I do to help?" Unless you spend some time thinking of potential answers, you may be at a loss. Below list some things a friend can do for you.**

_____

_____

10. Awkwardness is natural. Take the initiative to set the pace for friends who may not know what to do; be friendly and forthright; send the signal that you haven't shut them out.

11. Be prepared for a friend to be Jesus to you. What a difference one Jesus-motivated friend can make. I remember my first Thanksgiving as a single. Thanksgiving always had been special when we were married, but Thanksgiving 1975 was a day to grieve. I attended the community Thanksgiving service and tried to sing the four verses of "We Gather Together to Ask the Lord's Blessings." Blessings? What blessings? I was going through emotional open-heart surgery with no anesthesia. As I looked around the crowded, festive sanctuary, I saw couples everywhere. I was miserable. I was an associate dean at the college in this small town, and faculty members were present. If I could make it to the concluding choral "Amen," I would skip all the handshaking and go home.

That first lonely Thanksgiving

Two blocks from the church, I broke down in my car. I sobbed hysterically: ·God, where are you? I thought she would come home by now.

Since I had the largest oven on the block, my oven had been commandeered for roasting the communal turkey. The coordinator of the feast telephoned just as I walked in the door of the townhouse. When she heard my voice she asked, "Are you OK?" "No," I snarled. I am standing here in my kitchen, slobbering all over myself and trying to keep my heart in my chest wall. "Do you want Dan (her husband) to come over for a while?" she asked. "No!" I snapped. I didn't want Dan to see me crying, again.

A few minutes later, Dan walked in. "I am here to look at the turkey," he announced casually. *Well, here I am,* I thought. He walked to the oven and peered through the window; his bewildered look told me he didn't know a great deal about roasting turkeys. Still he announced, with great authority, "The turkey's not done!" He walked into my den and sat down on the other end of the couch and put his hands together and just sat there. I sobbed and he sat. I sobbed and he sat. "Maybe I'd better check it again . . . ." he said.

He returned to the couch, and we sat in silence. Dan didn't quote Romans 8:28 to me. He didn't offer any wiseisms from the power of possibility thinking movement. He simply sat there with me. Eventually he said, "I bet the turkey's done . . . let's go eat dinner." We carried the turkey down the street and gathered around a long table and thanked the Lord for His goodness and ate ourselves into oblivion.

I will never forget the Thanksgiving that Dan was Jesus to me.

That day is the strongest of all my Thanksgiving memories. I cannot tell you what I did last year or four years ago. But I will never forget the Thanksgiving that Dan was Jesus to me.

 Reflect on your file of friends. Who has been your equivalent of Dan? In the margin write some reflections about that friend.

Weekly Work

✎ **Continue to memorize this week's memory verses. How do they relate to the goal of loosening old attachments?**

About my friend—

_____

_____

_____

_____

Notes
[1]Elizabeth Harper Neeld, *Seven Choices: Taking the Steps to New Life After Losing Someone You Love,* (New York: Delta/Dell, 1990), 65-66.
[2]*Webster's Ninth New Collegiate Dictionary* (Springfield, MA: Merriam-Webster, 1983), 984.
[3]R. Scott Sullender, *Grief and Growth,* (Mahwah, NJ: Paulist Press, 1985), 40.
[4]Jason Towner, *Warm Reflections,* (Nashville: Broadman, 1977), 20.
[5]Lynn Gigy and Joan B. Kelly. "Reasons for Divorce: Perspectives of Divorcing Men and Women." *Journal of Divorce & Remarriage* 18(1/2): 173-175.
[6]Elizabeth Harper Neeld, *Seven Choices: Taking the Steps to New Life After Losing Someone You Love,* (New York: Delta/Dell, 1990), 65-66.
[7]Merriam-Webster, 995.
[8]Ganse Little. *The Interpreter's Bible,* Vol. II, (Nashville: Abingdon, 1953), 1059.
[9]Patti Roberts with Sherry Andrews. *Ashes to Gold,* (Waco, TX: Word, 1983), 148-149.
[10] Towner, 61.
[11]Little, 1059.

How respondents to the Gigy and Kelly survey ranked the factors listed on page 33, in order of importance to their decisions to divorce, with 1 being the factor a majority considered most important and 28 being the factor a majority considered least important: Statement 1 ranked 21 in importance; 2,20; 3,16; 4,3; 5,2; 6,11; 7,19; 8,15; 9,1; 10,4; 11,12; 12,17; 13,22; 14,24; 15,18; 16,23; 17,13; 18,14; 19,26; 20,5; 21,28; 22,27; 23,10; 24,25; 25,7; 26,6; 27,9; 28,8.

Revising the Assumptive World

This week's agenda:
You will learn to revise the old assumptive world of the way things are "supposed" to be.

> ## "I CAN'T LIVE THIS WAY"
>
> I still remember that night—three days into my separation—when I visited my friend David. Emotionally hemorrhaging, I asked, "David, how long am I going to hurt like this?"
>
> "Oh, about two years!" he answered.
>
> "Two years! What?" I exclaimed.
>
> "Well, that's been what I have observed in people who really get well after a divorce," he said.
>
> To that I answered, "I can't live this way for two weeks, let alone two years!"
>
> What did I need to remember in order to get through this difficult time? In this unit you will read about some things that helped me.

What you'll learn

This week you will—
- learn to confront some old assumptions;
- remember what we already know: that life isn't fair but that God is good;
- confront the injustices of the divorce process;
- explore the needs of individuals in the divorce/recovery process;
- look for God's telltale footprints in your divorce process and be reminded of His commitment to you.

What you'll study

Confronting Old Assumptions	Remembering What We Know	Confronting the Injustice	Exploring Our Needs	Looking for God's Footprints
DAY 1	DAY 2	DAY 3	DAY 4	DAY 5

Memory verse

This week's verse of Scripture to memorize—
Therefore I will not keep silent; I will speak out in the anguish of my spirit; I will complain in the bitterness of my soul.

—Job 7:11

DAY 1

Today's objective:
I will learn to confront the old assumptions about God.

In all this, Job did not sin by charging God with wrongdoing.

–Job 1:22

Are you still holding on to your integrity? Curse God and die!

–Job 2:9

Confronting Old Assumptions

Divorce happens! I long have wanted to print and sell bumper stickers stating that simple fact.[1] Divorce happens to a lot of people—probably 1,187,000 this year. We have heard the statistic that one out of two marriages will end in divorce; now some experts say that a more realistic figure may well be six out of ten![2]

"How could a good God let that happen?" That was a question I asked every day during my divorce. "How could a good God let/allow/permit divorce, especially to me?"

At many points in my divorce/recovery pilgrimage, my real crisis was theological: _where was God?_ I prayed, I fasted, I pleaded for His divine intervention. Although I never tried to call down His wrath on Jane, I did think about it. I hesitated, perhaps because of a story that people often hear about Abraham Lincoln. In the early days of the Civil War (and that is a good analogy to divorce) someone is said to have asked Lincoln if he thought God was on the side of the Union. "That's not the question," Lincoln rebutted. He said the question is "Are we on God's side?" Have you ever asked the question, "God, whose side are you on, anyway?"

That's why our memory verse is so important this week. The story of Job and his boils has been a powerful tale for thousands of years. People in all sorts of equivalents of "boils" have read the story of Job's miseries. The story was the background for a secular bestseller, _When Bad Things Happen to Good People._ The author of that book, Harold Kushner, challenged a major assumption: bad things are not supposed to happen to good people. Bad things are supposed to happen to bad people! How many times did my mom quote, "You will reap what you sow!"? _Well some people, like my ex, don't seem to be doing much reaping of bad sowing_, you snap.

Job lost his sheep, his oxen, his cattle, his lands, and his children. Not a pretty picture. See the Scripture appearing above and at left about what the Bible says about how Job responded.

✎ **Could what the Bible says of Job be said of you in your "all this"?**
❏ **Yes** ❏ **No** ❏ **Somewhat**

God points out to Satan that despite all the suffering Job "still maintains his integrity" (2:3). Did you have a point in your divorce that you thought things had gotten about as bad as they could get? In the margin box describe that moment. When things are about as bad as we assume they can get, things can get worse. In the second part of the margin box describe what happened then.

Next Job got boils from head to toe. It was so bad that Mrs. Job emotionally deserted him. See her words in Scripture appearing in the margin below. Job gets visitors. So great was his suffering that for seven days no one said a word. Then Job shared from his heart these words: "What I feared has come upon me; what I dreaded has happened to me" (3:25).

If you kept telling yourself that divorce cannot happen to you, you probably ignored a trail of hints your ex left—warning signals that you failed to notice.

**The first warning
signals were—**

_____

_____

_____

How I responded—

_____

_____

_____

Who, being innocent, has ever perished?
Where were the upright ever destroyed?
–Job 4:7

Therefore I will not keep silent; I will speak out in the anguish of my spirit; I will complain in the bitterness of my soul.

–Job 7:11

God is always able to
deal with our anger. God
never chides His children
for being children.

Or, you saw the signals but felt powerless to do anything about them. In the margin box describe the first warning signals in your divorce and how you responded to them. A guiding assumption at the time of the first signal often is: "Divorce can't happen to us. We're Christians."

The Jews assumed bad things did not happen to good people. So Eliphaz let Job have it. See his words in Job 4:7 (below left): This was his way of challenging Job's innocence. With friends like Eliphaz, who needs enemies? Rather than support Job, this friend accused him and said, "Now trouble comes to you, and you are discouraged; it strikes you, and you are dismayed" (4:5). Job gave Eliphaz a healthy response: see the second verse at left.

Some people assume we need to make the initiator "suffer." _Make her wish she had never thought about a divorce! Make him so sorry he'll . . .._ We assume that by coercion we can make people do the right thing.

This raises a key co-assumption: _It's risky to be angry at God_. I am convinced that a zillion divorced/ing individuals have unexpressed anger at God. Oh they may not keep silent in regard to their ex (and/or her/his attorney), but they will not speak out about their feelings toward God, who they believe failed them. Some internally fume, _God's got some explaining to do._

Becky tells this story: "It was not a pretty divorce. Small town. We were well known. And, I suppose everyone thought I was a fool to have ignored all his affairs. I knew about them. But he always came home to me, the kids; he always provided for us. Then he just threw everything to the wind, moved out and had a little second adolescence. The divorce was ugly. Finally it was over. He had stopped going to church, so the kids and I set about remaking our lives. One Sunday my middle child whispered, "Momma, Daddy's here." I immediately thought, _Well, good. If anybody needed some preaching, it was him._ Then my child added, "And _she's_ with him." It was all I could do to keep from walking out. Oddly, our pastor preached on the prodigal son. Then when Brother Ben offered the invitation, Ken (my ex) went forward. You could feel the buzz through the church. He was crying, and the pastor hugged him. Some of the deacons hugged him. I was livid. I know he was a member and all, but after all Ken had done, I hadn't seen any repentance in him."

✎ **What in Becky's story "leaps out" at you?**

_____

Was Ken the only person with whom she was angry?

_____

What counsel would you offer her?

_____

_____

We need to honestly express our feelings—including our anger—to God. Job expressed his anger. We need to follow his example.

➠ **Repeat the affirmation appearing at left.**

Remembering What We Know

I never have found carved in granite or marble or bronze the words, "Life is fair." In fact, I have listened to thousands of people contradict such a notion. As my mother often pointed out to me, rain falls on the just and the unjust.

Can we really expect to be immune from the realities of a fallen world? If we do not expect God to grant us immunity from wars, plagues, tornadoes, and earthquakes, can we expect immunity from divorce?

Today's objective:
I will remember that "life isn't fair but that God is good."

 Look at the statements below about God. Place a check in front of those with which you agree and an X in front of those with which you disagree.

_____ 1. God is omnipotent (all-powerful)
_____ 2. God is omniscient (all-knowing)
_____ 3. God's primary activity is that of a legislator and judge.
_____ 4. God issues commandments and calls for obedience.
_____ 5. God is eternal, changeless, the "unmoved mover."
_____ 6. God chose not to prevent my divorce.[7]

Have any of these beliefs changed as a result of your divorce? If so describe below which beliefs have changed.

_____

_____

_____

I believe that when we say, "Life is not fair!" we really are saying, "God is not fair!" For some of us, faith is supposed to be like a vaccination from the problems of life. I agreed with all of the statements except number 3.

If you make the Most High your dwelling—even the Lord, who is my refuge—then no harm will befall you, no disaster will come near your tent. For he will command his angels concerning you to guard you in all your ways.
                              –Psalm 91:9-11

 Read Psalm 91:9-11 appearing in the margin. Underline the key words of that great promise.

If you chose *if* and *then*, you are on track. We easily can memorize "no harm will befall you, no disaster will come." But what am I to do when my tent has just been flattened? Disaster was not supposed to come near my tent, let alone flatten it.

Some of the circumstances of life seem the perfect laboratory to test the Lord's "come-through"-ability. I grew up in a tradition that sang the chorus, "He never has failed me yet . . .. I have proven Him true, what He says, He will do. He never has failed me yet." Quite honestly I found that song difficult to sing during my divorce.

 Do you have difficulty singing or hearing certain songs? Below list them.

_____

He will call upon me, and I will answer him. I will be with him in trouble, I will deliver him and honor him.

–Psalm 91:15

✎ **Imagine you can sit down with the psalmist. Do you have some questions, based on your divorce experience, that you would like to ask about Psalm 91 (read another one of its verses appearing in the margin)? If so, write those questions below.**

_____

_____

You may have written that you think God has failed to answer you when you ask Him to break up your ex's new romantic relationship. You may think God has failed to deliver you from your custody battle for your children.

What C. S. Lewis wrote about widowhood and God is true in divorce. "Not that I am (I think) in much danger of ceasing to believe in God. The real danger is of coming to believe such dreadful things about Him. The conclusion I dread is not, 'So there's no God after all,' but 'So this is what God's really like. Deceive yourself no longer.'"[3]

We may well believe that this is some sort of test to examine the caliber of our faith. Circumstances can work under God's grace to make us strong. You may find yourself asking, Couldn't He find some other way? Is my divorce—particularly if I didn't anticipate it—more than a pop quiz to see how much I really know about faith or how much I will really depend on God?

No, Lewis contends, "God has not been trying an experiment on my faith or love in order to find out their quality. He knew it already." Then what is the point? "It was I who didn't (know their quality) . . .. He always knew that my temple was a house of cards. His only way of making me realize the fact was to knock it down."[4] God never tries to shush His children. Remember television's Archie Bunker ordering his wife Edith, "Would you stifle yourself!" God never asks His children to stifle themselves.

Weekly Work

✎ **Repeat three times this week's memory verse, Job 7:11.**

✎ **Say aloud the affirmation appearing at left.**

There is no wound that Jesus cannot heal; there is no history that Jesus cannot redeem.[5]

DAY 3

Today's objective:
I will confront the injustices of the process of divorce.

Confronting the Injustice

Injustices happen! When they do, they dispel the notion that "life is fair." Things in a divorce are supposed to work out a certain way but . . ., it doesn't always matter what divorce decrees say. Some exes snarl, "Make me live up to the agreements!" Some of us have concluded that the real injustice is that we have to hire lawyers to make our exes do what they promised to do.

One of the most powerful injustices in Scripture happened to a young princess, Tamar, daughter of King David. Turn to 2 Samuel 13 and read verses 1 through 21. The passage opens with young prince Amnon, the heir to the

Jewish throne, who has fallen in love with his half-sister. He wanted her so much he has become ill and cannot sleep.

Jonadab suggests that Amnon pretend to be ill. When King David hears that his firstborn son is sick, he will show up and eventually say, "Son, can I get something for you?" This being 3,000 years before pizza home delivery, Amnon is coached to suggest, "Some of that special bread of Tamar's would taste good." Jonadab's scheme works; David tells Tamar to "go . . . prepare some food for him." Amnon claims he is too ill to go to the kitchen, so he asks her to bring the food to his bedroom. When she does, the nightmare erupts. Amnon grabs her and says, "Come to bed with me." Tamar pleads for him not to rape her, but Scripture says, in a phrase many of us could use of our exes, "he refused to listen" (v. 14) and he raped her.

Listen to this phrase, "Then Amnon hated her with intense hatred" (v. 15). How many divorce courts have witnessed the intense hatred of someone who once loved the other party in the room? Listen to the next phrase, "he hated her more than he had loved her." Ah, yes, this sounds familiar, too. He attempts to "dispose" of this woman and says, "Get up and get out!" Tamar says no. Then "he called his personal servant and said, 'Get this woman out of here and bolt the door after her'" (v. 17). Tamar has a name, a title, a relationship to him, yet he dismisses her as "this woman." So she is thrown out of his royal chambers. She weeps profusely, tears her clothing, and slowly stumbles to her quarters.

"I wept until I thought my insides were going to fall out. I sobbed until my face swelled up and my stomach hurt. I thought I was going to die."

✎ **Take a moment and reread 2 Samuel 13:1-19. Identify three points in this account that resemble what you have experienced during the divorce process. Do you see any resemblance between divorce and rape?**

1. _____

2. _____

3. _____

You may have written that you have seen these similarities: *My ex hasn't listened to my pleas. I have been thrown out of my house. I feel that I have been tricked like Tamar was.* Watch what happens when she runs into her brother Absalom, Amnon's half-brother. We expect him to say, "What in the world has happened to you?" and to comfort her. His words are: "Has that Amnon, our brother, been with you? Be quiet now, my sister, he is your brother. Don't take this thing to heart."

✎ **Has anyone discovered your emotional/spiritual dishevelment and yet failed to offer you comfort? Describe the response they gave.**

_____

_____

I believe Tamar's story has real relevance to divorce:
1. Tamar suffered three rapes:
  A. Her body had been raped.
  B. Her reputation had been raped. Why did Amnon ask the servant to "put

her out and bolt the door"? Because he knew that servants share bits and pieces of "behind the scenes" with other servants? He was attempting to put a spin on the situation that would tarnish Tamar as an "initiator."

C. Her future had been raped. It did not matter that she was a virgin daughter of the king. The rape cost her her virginity. Without virginity in Jewish society she never could marry. Tamar had every right to snarl, "It isn't fair!"

2. What had Tamar lost? Four things come to mind.

A. Tamar lost a physical part of herself: her virginity and her sense of innocence. What have you lost in the divorce process? Maybe not your virginity but maybe your sense of innocence, particularly if you discovered marital infidelity.

B. Tamar lost her self-esteem. Tamar, no doubt, felt good about herself. She had a wonderful future. But who would want her now?

C. Tamar lost her self-identity. She was a daughter of the King of Israel. I doubt that she had to worry about where her next meal was coming from. The future was bright: she knew that eventually she would marry—and marry well. Her father would plan a royal wedding for her.

D. Tamar may have lost her belief in God. How could the God of the 91st Psalm—the God who promised "no disaster will come near your tent"— let this happen? She had only done what her father had asked her to do. She was simply in the wrong place at the wrong time. In the margin box compare your experience of divorce with Tamar's experience in the four categories listed in the box.

3. How did Tamar grieve? Grief is a very individualistic response, conditioned on a lot of factors. Still, most of us, according to Dr. Alan Wolfelt, select from the following menu of grief behaviors.

A. **Postponers.** Some of us do not have time to deal adequately with all of the issues, so we deal with the most pressing. "I have three children to feed," Karen explained. Maybe someday we'll get around to our grief.

B. **Displacers.** Displacers stay so busy, often with keeping a roof over their head, feeding the children, keeping the wolves from the door, that they don't have time to think about the deeper issues of the divorce or work on recovery.

C. **Replacers.** Wolfelt argues, "Women grieve, men replace." His thesis is supported by the statistics that 75 percent of men remarry within 14 months of a divorce. Some people get over a divorce by premature promises and hasty second marriages.

D. **Minimizers.** People love to exchange "tales of the trail." If you say you had no children or weren't married long, expect someone to minimize your pain. We are tempted to discount your divorce pain and to exaggerate our own.

E. **Somaticizers.** Some of us try to ignore our divorce pain only to find it appear in slightly different forms of somatic complaints (physical symptoms of emotional pain): migraine headaches, backaches, colitis, ulcers. Some people think that they suffer painful physical conditions only to discover that unhealed personal relationships are contributing greatly to their pain. The body will go to great lengths to get your attention.[6]

✎ Circle the categories that describe how you grieve. Put a star by which category best describes your approach to your divorce. Explain why.

A future clouded

I feel I have lost—

Physically: _____

_____

_____

Self-esteem: _____

_____

_____

Self-identity: _____

_____

_____

Belief in God: _____

_____

_____

_____

There is no wound that Jesus cannot heal; There is no history that Jesus cannot redeem..

DAY 4

Today's objective:
I will explore my needs as an individual in the divorce-recovery process.

Few of us have known the luxury of having someone who will listen to us until the end of the sentence.

Weekly Work

✎ In the margin write what this week's memory verse means to you.

➡ Repeat the affirmation appearing in the margin.

Exploring Our Needs

What are the needs of individuals who divorce has deeply wounded? We have three basic needs.

Need One: To express to someone the reality of what has happened—someone who will listen all the way to the end of the sentences and who will not interrupt the silences.

✎ **Contrast the memory verse for the week with Absalom's words to Tamar, "Be quiet now . . . Don't take this thing to heart." Whose advice are you more likely to take?** ❏ Job's ❏ Absalom's ❏ Unsure

✎ **The paragraph above uses the term "listen all the way to the end of the sentences." Who has listened to you in this manner? Name your "ears."**

_____

Did you have an empty blank? One assumption we have about grief is that the key people in our lives will listen and will be there for us in our time of desperate need. That doesn't always happen. During the divorce some people have listened, but they offer easy one-two-threes to encourage us to get on with our life. Some selectively listened, but their minds already were made up.

Indeed, the value of listening to stories is one of the principles behind this format for divorce recovery. Many divorce-recovery programs present a body of material related to the "stages of grief." Small group discussions follow this. That is good for 90 minutes. But what about the other 9,990 minutes of the week? This workbook is a way to deal with those "in-between" times.

Divorce recovery can be like a verbal quilt made up of snatches from all types of experiences. The reason people like Tamar need to express the reality is that some of the pieces initially make no sense. Only a skilled and patient listener can help us see what is hidden in the story and needs to be aired.

Need Two: To tolerate the emotional suffering while nurturing oneself physically, emotionally and spiritually—One night in an emergency room, a woman demanded treatment for "a broken heart." "Can you give me something for the pain?" I never wandered into an emergency room with my broken heart, but I have barged into the homes of friends and asked, "Can you give me something for the pain?" The world offers some readily available anesthetics to relieve the pain of a broken heart: alcohol; drugs—sometimes physician-dispensed; promiscuity; wild-timing: partying; spending sprees. If I can keep myself preoccupied and dulled to the realities, I won't have to deal with them. But like all anesthesia, these wear off.

Think back to those early days of your divorce. How did you initially confront your pain?

_____

Did you stop using this anesthesia for any particular reason? Why?

_____

Sadly, some people almost engage in a worse-case self-fulfilling prophecy. They set out to finish what an ex initiated. They spin emotionally "out of control"—only a matter of time until the big crash.

Most of us are not good at tolerating; the more we try, the more intense the pain becomes. That is one reason so many people—men, in particular—race into a rebound relationship. Sadly, they marry in such an emotional fog they cannot see the rocky, jagged coasts of potential danger in the new relationship. We want instant tea, coffee, pizza, whatever. It is only logical that such a society produce instant relationships—and instant cures for pain.

I still remember that night—three days into my separation—when I visited my friend David. Emotionally hemorrhaging, I asked, "David, how long am I going to hurt like this?" "Oh, about two years!" he answered. "Two years! What?" I exclaimed. "Well, that's been what I have observed in people who really get well after a divorce," he said. To that I answered, "I can't live this way for two weeks, let alone two years!" I wish I had a magic wand, a formula, a potion, a video that could zap all the emotional pain, particularly of the newly divorced. But I would not be doing them a favor. As they say at my health club, "No pain—no gain!" Pain is a vital ingredient in healing.

Pain is a vital ingredient in healing.

Need Three: To convert the incident from presence to memory—It's so tempting to hit the stop, rewind, replay buttons on a tape player in rapid sequence. Over and over and over, until the cassette is worn out. Or, on a VCR to punch the still button and freeze the incident on the screen of our hearts. So tempting to run the sequences in slow, slow motion—reliving the pain. Healing does not happen without our cooperation. In autographing my book, _I Wish Someone Understood My Divorce_, I often have written, "Tomorrow begins today!" Today can be—if you leave the rewind/still buttons alone—the first day of your healing.

 Think about a windshield and a rear-view mirror of a car. What is the purpose of each?

_____

Did you write: _to see where you are going and to see where you've been?_ Good. Think a moment about the size of these two necessities for safe auto driving. Why is the windshield so large? Why is the rear-view mirror so small? In the margin box write your answer.

Now, in your emotions, which is larger, your windshield or your rear-view mirror? We often reverse the sizes. We have rear-view mirrors the size of our windshields to see everything that ever has hurt us, yet we try to peer through a tiny windshield at the future to which God is calling us. In recovery we need our rear-view and forward perspectives to be in correct proportions.

Why is the rear-view mirror so small and the windshield so large?

_____

_____

_____

_____

_____

Secondly, we need to invite Jesus to be "Lord of our memories." I like to browse in poster shops and art galleries. Sometimes, in revisiting a gallery, I notice that a particular painting has been removed for cleaning or for exhibit elsewhere. We all have exhibit spaces in our hearts. There on the walls, sometimes in bright lights, sometimes in dim, hang the "incidents" of our lives. Sometimes we avoid certain galleries completely.

➡ **Close your eyes and breathe deeply. Picture that exhibit hall in your heart. Browse through some of the well-lit galleries. See Jesus there. Imagine Jesus turning toward a dark room but you hesitate. You don't want to go any further. Jesus speaks, "Does this room bother you?" "Oh yes," you reply. Jesus walks to a particular painting and you wince in pain. "This one bothers you, doesn't it?" You nod. Jesus lifts the painting from the wall, and now you see blank space. Jesus walks from the room and returns with a new painting. "Now look!" There hangs a painting for the new you.**

Jesus wants to be the curator of the galleries of our memories, but we have to agree to His curatorship. It may take a while for Him to weed out the bad paintings and to replace them with masterpieces, but if we cooperate, He will do just that.

✎ **Think of a particular bad painting (memory) that you want to discard. In the margin describe it. This can be a memory of something that you said or something that was said to you; this can be something you did or something that was done to you.**

➡ **Invite Jesus to become Lord of this memory and do with it what He will.**

Weekly Work

➡ **Repeat the affirmation appearing at left.**

Looking for God's Footprints

How can you look for God's footprints in the midst of your divorce?

1. Remember that God cares about you. In the midst of a reality called divorce, God still cares. That's difficult for us to comprehend in the midst of our pain. Paul phrased a question that remains on the front of our spirits. It begins "Who shall separate us from the love of Christ?" (Romans 8:35). Read this entire verse appearing in the margin on the next page and answer the questions below.

✎ **What does Paul say will not separate us from the love of God? In the spaces below write the words.**

_____ _____ _____ _____

_____ _____ _____

A bad memory I want to discard—
_____
_____
_____
_____
_____
_____

There is no wound that Jesus cannot heal; There is no history that Jesus cannot redeem.

DAY 5

Today's objective:
I will look for God's telltale footprints in my divorce process and will be reminded of His commitment to me.

Who shall separate us from the love of Christ? Shall trouble or hardship or persecution or famine or nakedness or danger or sword?

–Romans 8:35

No, in all these things we are more than conquerors through him who loved us.

–Romans 8:37

To underscore the point, now go back through and scratch out each of the words you wrote in.

Dare I add one: divorce? Go back and reread this list but insert divorce in the blank spot to the right of the last word in the list. Certainly, divorce overlaps some of these factors. It definitely counts as trouble and hardship. It leads to a famine, maybe not by some standards but nevertheless emotional starvation. Nakedness is not just physical nudity but also emotional nakedness—when we have been stripped of every shred of our dignity. Now read the precious promise appearing in the second verse at left.

Conquerors? In divorce? Yes, in that we determine that we will survive divorce not just somehow but in a victorious way. We can choose not to respond in ways that would challenge the integrity of our faith. We can vow to seek in this divorce a way for God to be glorified.

2. God hurts, too. One of my favorite choruses when I was a child went like this: "God can do anything, anything, anything. God can do anything but fail." That verse came back to haunt me rather than comfort me during my divorce. I had been sure God would not let the divorce happen. But now on the kitchen table lay a piece of paper from the County of Transylvania, North Carolina, which in my limited judgment, indicted God. He had failed to come through on time.

God is as brokenhearted as we are about what happens to us.

Years after the divorce, I found comforting words from my friend, David Seamands. If only they had been available in July, 1976, in my time of need. Seamands wrote: "The first step in our healing is to realize that God understands where the feelings are coming from and is as brokenhearted about it as we are. He wants to work with us in freeing us from them."[7]

 Go back and circle key words or phrases in Seamands' quote. In the space below write how you respond to them.

R. Scott Sullender asks us to consider a side of God I believe the divorced have to see in order to survive. He writes: "There is another view of God—that is, as companion, as friend and fellow sojourner with each human being. This God is involved in the world, and, therefore, knows intimately the pain and suffering of all living beings. This is the tender side of God, the feeling side of God, the God who listens to prayers and who suffers with and for people. This God feels what we feel, weeps as we weep. This God is our comforter who helps us in our trials, rather than the one who brings on our trials. This God is the forgiving parent, rather than the punishing parent. This God is involved in the process of life, rather than watching from above it. This God is the one who is still creating, molding and fashioning the world, through the lives and actions of believers."[8]

God as fellow sufferer

Sullender talks about personal friends whose unwelcomed divorce destroyed their fragile faiths. He writes, "When it became apparent that God did not 'promise a rose garden,' they gave up the notion of God with their baby clothes and acne medicine. Their old image of God died, but in their haste for easy answers, they overlooked the God who shared their pain, 'God as Fellow-Sufferer,' the God who transforms pain into new life."[9]

How long, O Lord? Will you forget me forever? How long will you hide your face from me? How long must I wrestle with my thoughts and every day have sorrow in my heart? How long will my [ex] triumph over me?

–Psalm 13:1-2

My God, my God, why have you forsaken me? Why are you so far from saving me, so far from the words of my groaning?

–Psalm 22:1

About the ninth hour Jesus cried out in a loud voice, *"Eloi, Eloi, lama sabachthani?"*—which means, "My God, my God, why have you forsaken me?"

–Matthew 27:46

Can a mother forget the baby at her breast and have no compassion on the child she has borne? Though she may forget, I will not forget you! See, I have engraved you on the palms of my hands.

–Isaiah 49:15-16

 What would it take for you to change your view of God, say, through what you are learning in this divorce recovery process?

_____

3. No circumstances of life will defeat God. In the early months of my divorce, I looked desperately for answers to buoy my faith as it floundered. Here was my dilemma: Jane had vowed to love me forever. Jane had stopped loving me. Then couldn't God stop loving me, too? And I had moments that God seemed about ten zillion miles away. In those times, I sought the Psalms that were laced with darkness, such as Psalm 13:1-2 and Psalm 22:1, which appear at left. I felt better knowing that Jesus, when He assumed He had been forgotten, quoted this dark Psalm, as Matthew 27:46 reports.

One afternoon as I read C. S. Lewis' *A Grief Observed*, I found insight from this great apologist's struggle as he wrestled with the dark Psalms. "When I lay these questions before God I get no answer. But a rather special sort of 'No answer.' It is not the locked door. It is more like a silent, certainly not uncompassionate, gaze. As though He shook His head not in refusal but waiving the question. Like, 'Peace, child; you don't understand.'"[10] I have learned that God can handle my "Why?" questions. I just have to be prepared for "no response" on my timetable.

4. God does not forsake/forget His children. Read Isaiah 49:15 at left for a wonderful insight into God's tender side. So many of us have a tendency to see God's will as a straight line. Once we are detoured, we think we must come back to the original line. I think it is more like a network (maze); and in eternity's day when we watch the videotapes of our lives, we will be surprised to see His will weaving itself through this turn and that turn.

5. God gives us strength to face our circumstances. God generally gives strength in daily dosages; like manna, strength cannot be stored. In the words of the great hymn classic, "Great Is Thy Faithfulness": *Great is thy faithfulness! Morning by morning new mercies I see; All I have needed Thy hand hath provided. Great is thy faithfulness, Lord, unto me.*[11]

The song says *all I have needed* but not *all I have wanted.* Listen to this passage from the third verse: "Strength for today and bright hope for tomorrow." God gives us strength to face our circumstances—even the circumstances we'd rather pass on or sit out. Simply, God gives us strength today. Rarely ahead of time.

Read this quote from Harold Kushner: "To the person who asks 'what good is God? Who needs religion, if these things happen to good people and bad people alike?', I would say that God may not prevent the calamity, but He gives us the strength and the perseverance to overcome it. Where else do we get these qualities which we did not have before?[12] God does not say, "Oh, Joe looks like he's got a lot of faith and spunk. Let's allow an unwanted divorce to whack him upside his reality and see how he handles it." No, God says, "Joe's wife has left him; he's going to need strength today."

6. God brings people into our lives to help us with our new realities. God may not keep the divorce from happening, but He will work overtime to see that you do not feel "alone, abandoned, or judged." God does not comfort you in this divorce so that you will quit bugging Him in prayer. He comforts you so that you will be able to share that comfort with others who are hurting. As Kushner concluded, "God inspires people to help other people who have been hurt by life."[13]

7. God leaves footprints in our lives. Look for them. In 1910, Christians in the South were singing a wonderful new gospel song "He Keeps Me Singing," written by Georgia preacher Luther B. Bridgers. Perhaps you've sung his spirited "There's within my heart a melody, Jesus whispers sweet and low; 'Fear not, I am with thee; peace be still,' In all of life's ebb and flow."[14]

Sharing comfort

Bridgers wrote both words and music presumably after the tragic loss of his wife and children who were burned to death in a house fire while he was conducting a revival in Kentucky. The fourth verse says: "Tho' sometimes He leads thro' waters deep, Trials fall across the way, Tho' sometimes the path seems rough and steep, See His footprints all the way."[15] Out of great pain, Bridgers could see footprints. Out of your great pain, know that God is there.

There is no wound that Jesus cannot heal; There is no history that Jesus cannot redeem.

Weekly Work

✎ **In the margin write the memory verse in your own words.**

➠ **Repeat the affirmation appearing at left.**

Notes

[1]U.S. Bureau of the Census. *Statistical Abstract of the United States: 1993*. 113th ed. Washington: U.S. Government Printing Office, 1993, 73.

[2]Michael J. McManus. "Churches: Wedding Factories or Marriage Savers." *National & International Religion Report* Special Supplement (Nov. 1, 1993), P.O. Box 21433, Roanoke, VA 24018, (703) 989-7500. Used by permission.

[3]C. S. Lewis, *A Grief Observed*, (New York: Bantam, 1976), 5.

[4]Lewis, 61.

[5]Linda Quanstrom, "And Then There Was One." message, First Church of the Nazarene, Kansas City, Missouri, 3 February 1992.

[6]Alan Wolfelt, *Death and Grief: A Guide for Clergy*, (Muncie, IN: Accelerated Development, 1988), 115-120; as well as from a lecture by Alan Wolfelt, Olathe, Kansas, February 10, 1991.

[7]David A. Seamands, *Healing Grace*, (Wheaton, IL: Victor Books, 1988), 157.

[8]R. Scott Sullender, *Grief and Growth: Pastoral Responses for Emotional and Spiritual Growth*, (New York: Paulist Press, 1985), 188.

[9]Ibid, 189.

[10]Lewis, 81.

[11]Thomas O. Chisholm, "Great Is Thy Faithfulness," ©1923. Renewal 1951 by Hope Publishing Co., Carol Stream, IL 60188. All rights reserved. Used by permission.

[12]Harold S. Kushner, *When Bad Things Happen to Good People*, (New York: Schocken, 1981), 141.

[13]Ibid., 139.

[14]Luther Bridgers, "He Keeps Me Singing," *The Baptist Hymnal*, (Nashville: Convention Press, 1991), 425.

[15]William J. Reynolds, *Hymns of Our Faith*, (Nashville: Broadman Press, 1964), 210.

Readjusting to New Realities

This week's agenda:
You will readjust to the new realities in your life.

LEARNING TO COPE

Camille recalled: "I awakened several mornings to find myself hugging a pillow or with my hand wrapped around a pillow. I thought this was positive proof that I was losing my mind. I was afraid to share this with anyone, including my counselor. What would they think?"

The woman who had a lot to do with breaking up Sara's marriage called Sara and asked, "How have you managed to remain a lady all these years?" Even in the midst of a messy divorce, Sara chose again and again to conduct herself with integrity.

How have these two individuals adjusted to the new realities in their lives as a result of divorce? Within this unit we'll explore these new realities and offer biblical solutions.

What you'll learn

This week you will—
• review God's will on intimacy and sexuality;
• gain insight into daily survival and coping skills;
• consider five strategies for dealing with loneliness;
• redefine responsibility;
• to investigate forgiveness.

What you'll study

God's Will on Intimacy, Sexuality	A Reality Called Loneliness	Loneliness (Part II)	Redefining Responsibility	Redefining Responsibility (Part II)
DAY 1	DAY 2	DAY 3	DAY 4	DAY 5

Memory verses

This week's verse of Scripture to memorize—
For the grace of God that brings salvation has appeared to all men. It teaches us to say "No" to ungodliness and worldly passions, and to live self-controlled, upright and godly lives in this present age.

—Titus 2:11-12

God's Will on Intimacy, Sexuality

DAY

1

Today's objective:
I will review God's standards and plans for intimacy and sexuality.

When we tune into an afternoon talk show, read one of the magazines in the grocery check-out line, or flip through the evening TV channels, we find that sex is the topic *du jour*. What about you and the issue of sex? What is or is not going on sexually with you? As you consider your situation as a divorcing, recently divorced, or long-time divorced person, how are you adjusting to your new reality?

✎ **Below put a check in the box beside the term which describes your approach to sex at this point. (We will not ask you to share this with the group.)**

❑ Hot and bothered
❑ Celibate and confused
❑ Reluctantly celibate
❑ Quasi-celibate

❑ Sexually frustrated
❑ Uninterested in sex
❑ Struggling

Owning up to where we are is a healthy start in dealing with this delicate issue of sexuality and intimacy. A couple of realities compound the issue. First, some of us are not highly interested in sex; even in marriage, sex was sporadic. On the other hand, some of us were accustomed to regular sexual expression in marriage. Because we did not anticipate the divorce, we feel that someone slammed on the sex brakes. Others of us feel rejected. Some of us have struggled; we're celibate today, uncelibate tomorrow. Some of us carry enormous loads of guilt. Let's look at these considerations:

Slamming on the brakes

1. Attitudes shape our realities. Sex doesn't just happen. Attitudes, some of which are based more on faulty reasoning than on a biblical faith, precede it.

✎ **Place a check in the appropriate column for each attitude listed below.**

Agree	Disagree	Unsure	
❑	❑	❑	1. No marriage/no sex! Plain and simple.
❑	❑	❑	2. If no one gets hurt, and no one knows, and we practice "safe sex," it's not as wrong.
❑	❑	❑	3. "Everybody's doing it . . . ."
❑	❑	❑	4. It depends on the situation.
❑	❑	❑	5. Celibacy is old-fashioned.
❑	❑	❑	6. A man has to have sex.
❑	❑	❑	7. Sex and intimacy are synonyms.
❑	❑	❑	8. What I do sexually is nobody's business but my own.
❑	❑	❑	9. Celibacy is a good ideal, but God understands if we mess up.
❑	❑	❑	10. Sex is not wrong if two people really love each other.
❑	❑	❑	11. I feel condemned by some of my sexual choices.
❑	❑	❑	12. I want to do what's right, but I am pretty weak as far as sex is concerned.

Look over your answers. A big difference exists between what we do and say. And it's not as if discipline is a new issue. Look in the margin on the next page

For what I want to do I do not do; but what I hate I do.

–Romans 7:15

For what I do is not the good I want to do; no, the evil I do not want to do—this I keep on doing.

–Romans 7:19

to see what Paul, a single adult—perhaps even a single-again—wrote in Romans 7:15. Then look at verse 19 which appears below it. Paul's words do not refer to his sexuality, but the principle of struggle applies to our sexual temptations.

 In the context of sexuality, write below a modern-day paraphrase of Paul's words.

_____

_____

You may have written something like this: *I know that being sexually active is not best for me, but I struggle with temptation. I hate to violate God's commands regarding sexuality, but I have difficulty putting on the brakes.*

2. Advice is plentiful; wisdom is sparse. The culture will tell you, "Do it. You're an adult; you have these needs." Suppose you know your ex is not celibate. Does that make it easier or more difficult for you to be celibate? I often tell people, "Guard your heart." I bought wonderful German "heart" Christmas ornaments. They are very delicate. They have no bounce-ability! If you drop them, no more ornament. Well, more hearts get broken through inappropriate sexual behavior than in any other way.

Last week we talked about a prince named Amnon who was in love with his sister, Tamar. Remember, he wasn't sleeping too well. Some of us, particularly if we describe ourselves as sexually frustrated, understand that. But he took advice from Jonadab. Jonadab's advice started Amnon in the wrong direction, and he destroyed a princess' life and future. Some advice is worth about what you paid for it. To whom are you listening?

3. Anarchy is rampant. Get a bumper sticker made saying, "Celibate and Proud of It!" and watch the reactions. We live in a time of sexual anarchy: anything goes, of course, "as long as no one gets hurt." But a lot of counselors and therapists are making their house payments and putting braces on their kids' teeth by listening to the sexually scarred and the sexually burned out.

Following the Owner's Manual

Thou shalt not commit adultery.
Exodus 20:14, KJV

For this is the will of God, even your sanctification, that ye should abstain from fornication.
1 Thessalonians 4:3, KJV

Maybe we'd have less struggle if our bodies would not function sexually unless we were married. No sexual stimulation/no temptation. But God endowed us with this incredible capacity for sexual expression; as with all good gifts, we're better off when we follow the Owner's Manual. (See the verses appearing at left.) And in the Owner's Manual God has said no to sex outside marriage, either through fornication (any kind of non-marital sexual intercourse) or adultery (sexual intercourse by a married person with a person other than one's spouse.) As the Creator of sex He knew that using sex outside His purposes could wound, hurt, and destroy.

 How are you dealing with this topic? Maybe it's a little too sensitive. Take a moment and describe how you react so far to this subject matter.

_____

_____

_____

Then write a prayer, asking the Lord to help you apply this material to your life. On a separate sheet of paper finish this thought.

Lord, in my own life, I need _____

We can pray about anything, including about our sexuality.

Someone I was counseling talked all around the edge of this topic. Finally, he admitted that he was having difficulty dealing with his sex drives. "Have you talked to God about this?" I asked. "To God?!" he answered incredulously. "You can't talk to God about sex." I replied, "Why not? He already knows . . .." "Oh, no!" he replied, covering his face with his hands. "I'm in big trouble." That's the way a lot of us are. We've talked to a lot of people about our sexuality but never to the One who created our sexuality.

 Read closely the words of the following hymn, "What A Friend We Have In Jesus." Highlight words that "leap out" at you when you apply this hymn to your sexuality.

*What a Friend we have in Jesus,
All our sins and griefs to bear!
What a privilege to carry
Everything to God in prayer.
Oh, what peace we often forfeit,
Oh, what needless pain we bear,
All because we do not carry
Everything to God in prayer.*[1]

You may have highlighted *griefs to bear, everything, needless pain we bear*. It's amazing that hymnwriter Joseph Scriven listed *everything* twice. Everything means anything. We should be able to pray the landscape of our lives. In our memory verses Paul says for us to be upright, not uptight! Paul does not demand that we become modern-day Shakers and reject all sexual activity of any kind, nor does he suggest that we find the nearest monastery and sign up. "In this present age" that the memory verses mentions means in your zip code, today. Agenda 8 devotes five entire days' worth of study to this important area.

Weekly Work

➠ **Repeat three times this week's memory verses, Titus 2:11-12. Begin to memorize them**

DAY 2

Today's objective:
I will respond appropriately to loneliness, a reality in the life of everyone.

A Reality Called Loneliness

Years ago Bobby Vinton popularized a song called, "Lonely, I'm Mr. Lonely." Many divorced people can recognize the reality in that title, for these reasons:

1. Divorced people have a zillion reasons for feeling lonely. Daily life in a marriage revolves around an intricate network of rituals and themes such as leisure, seasons, chores, child nurturing; the longer one has been married, the more habitualized are these rituals. Something about the repetition of these events and occurrences bonds people that participate in them to each other in a way that becomes very much a part of the individuals' identities. Simply, when the rituals fail to occur, one or both partners recognize that something is amiss. Each solo-performed ritual reminds: you are single!

 Below, in the list of rituals that are common in marriage, put a check in the appropriate column.

Soloing a habit

I Miss/I Do Not Miss
- ❑ ❑ 1. doing household maintenance chores together
- ❑ ❑ 2. doing laundry or the dishes together
- ❑ ❑ 3. jointly preparing meals
- ❑ ❑ 4. attending church services together
- ❑ ❑ 5. reviewing bills together/reconciling checkbook
- ❑ ❑ 6. watching TV at night together
- ❑ ❑ 7. shopping together
- ❑ ❑ 8. watching videos together
- ❑ ❑ 9. praying together
- ❑ ❑ 10. sleeping together
- ❑ ❑ 11. having sex together

You may find yourself in the midst of one of these routines—say, balancing your checkbook—and suddenly be reminded of the times when the two of you balanced the checkbook. Without knowing why, you can become depressed while you perform this routine. Has this ever happened to you? ❑ Yes ❑ No.

2. Sometimes we are lonely for no reason. Just because.

3. Loneliness may be tied to sleeping patterns. Many single-agains make it through the day with no problem, but they come unglued at night. At bedtime that aspect of aloneness reannounces itself. Perhaps you have just become single again and are having real trouble sleeping single in a double or king-sized bed.

 In the list below check the descriptions that apply to you.

Yes No
- ❑ ❑ Do you have trouble going to sleep?
- ❑ ❑ Do you sleep in the same bed as when you were married?
- ❑ ❑ Do you initially go to sleep only to awaken later and be unable to go back to sleep?
- ❑ ❑ Do you count sheep?
- ❑ ❑ Have you rearranged the bedroom furniture?
- ❑ ❑ Do you still sleep on "your side" of the bed?

How is your bedtime routine as a single different than it was as a married adult? Write your answers in the margin box.

Camille recalled: "I awakened several mornings to find myself hugging a pillow or with my hand wrapped around a pillow. I thought this was positive proof that I was losing my mind. I was afraid to share this with anyone, including my counselor. What would they think?"

Adjustments in sleeping

Such responses illustrate the deep emotional pain through which the recently divorced may go, particularly if the divorce was an ambush or surprise. It took me a while to learn to sleep alone.

As a married adult I—

_____

_____

_____

As a single adult I—

_____

_____

_____

I am worn out from groaning; all night long I flood my bed with weeping and drench my couch with tears.

–Psalm 6:6

O My God, I cry in the daytime, but thou hearest not; and in the night season, and am not silent.

–Psalm 22:2, KJV

I prevented the dawning of the morning, and cried.

–Psalm 119:147, KJV

When you lie down, you will not be afraid; when you lie down, your sleep will be sweet.

–Proverbs 3:24

For he grants sleep to those he loves.

–Psalm 127:2

Some things I fear—

_____

_____

_____

Many single adults have been disturbed—even freaked-out—by dreaming about the former mate. Some of us will have particularly vivid sex-oriented dreams of intimacy with our ex. These dreams can be most troubling. But guess what? Scripture has a lot to say about sleep and grief. See the three verses at left. In the night David, the psalmist, no longer was king—he was just another man who needed rest. I can relate to David's sleeplessness. These verses comfort me to realize that 3,000 years ago, someone dared put his "Sleepless in Israel" experiences into writing and that God has preserved them to help me in my time of trouble and sexual frustration.

3. We cannot deny loneliness. Some ignore or deny the need exists. But it is natural, especially after years of marriage. The best response is to recognize it.

A. Invite the Lord. A counselor suggested that nightly I pray the following: *Lord, I've been alright up to now. But, in this moment, I need help to go upstairs and to go to sleep. I do not have resources to deal with my need. Please help me.* God answered that request. Remember in yesterday's work, we talked about carrying "everything to God in prayer"? Sleeping patterns definitely are included in "everything."

B. Remember the promises that appear in the fourth and fifth verses at left. Do you see any asterisks indicating that these promises are made to people except for those going through a divorce? God wants to bring you sleep.

C. Name your fears. We are afraid, particularly at bedtime, of such matters as what a violence-threatening ex might do, the impact of the divorce on our children, being unable to pay our bills, our dwindling bank balance, or the shakiness of our job. In the margin box at left, name your fears. Again, because we are sleeping in a bed where possibly we have had sex, feelings lying deep in the dark canyons of our soul naturally surface. The devil even may ask, "Why are you living like a nun/a monk? You need sex." Don't be surprised if sexual longing arrives like a pounding surf.

D. Guard what you put into your head and heart before you go to bed. Some parents deny a child's request to watch a certain movie by saying, "No! It will give you nightmares." Adults can have nightmares, too. Avoid these things:
- "Heavy" porn. The popularization of the VCR has brought questionable movies into our homes and sometimes into our bedrooms. Someone else's sin, graphically portrayed, will not be edifying to us.
- "Soft" porn. Some of us never would rent or watch an X- or R-rated movie, but the "bodice-ripper" romance novels are available readily. Some divorced women read these incessantly. We easily can read ourselves into sexual arousal as well.
- Just before bedtime is no time to schedule a pity party, but it is a wonderful time to schedule a praise party to thank God for the day and for His love and for His generous provision for your needs.

Weekly Work

➡ **Stop and pray, asking God to keep you so close to Him that you can turn all of your anxious moments over to Him.**

➡ **Repeat a special verse for today's emphasis:**
"Do not be anxious about anything, but in everything, by prayer and petition, with thanksgiving, present your requests to God. And the peace of God, which transcends all understanding, will guard your hearts and your minds in Christ Jesus" (Philippians 4:6-7). Dare we add our sleep to what Jesus will guard?

Today's objective:
I will continue to respond to loneliness, a reality in the life of every divorced person.

Loneliness (Part II)

In the last segment we primarily examined sexual loneliness. In some marriages, because of the tension or the active reality of an "other" in your spouse's life, sex already had tapered off.

Today, we want to focus on the other dimensions of active loneliness. Turn back to page 61 and find the list of marital rituals; quickly scan them. Little things ignite long-soaked resentment. Loneliness leads to boredom, and boredom can lead to sin.

Fitted sheets. This was my "igniter." Although I had no problem doing laundry, I never could get fitted sheets with those round edges to fold properly. Although Jane had repeatedly demonstrated the folding technique, I never mastered it. As a newly divorced person, fitted sheets could send me into a rage. Small, insignificant thing, but it was so symbolic. What is your igniter? Consider these aspects of loneliness:

1. A big difference exists between being lonely and being alone. As a writer, I need lots of alone time. Little noises can create havoc with my concentration. To varying degrees all of us need aloneness; indeed, one of the unfair aspects of single parenting is that the active parent seldom gets enough—if any—alone time. Even when the kids are with the other parent, you have about a half-zillion chores to complete before the children return. Time for yourself? That's a luxury.

✎ **Below describe the last time you were totally alone.**

_____

_____

If you had to label that time in one word, that one word would be

_____

A fear of aloneness

2. Loneliness is a decision. I may not have chosen to be lonely, but I make the decision to remain lonely. Some divorced individuals cannot stand being alone; in fact some never are alone. Even a noisy, smoked-filled bar, they reason, beats four off-white walls. But often the divorced person has to deal with the reality of four off-white walls with a green carpet in a rental apartment that pretty much looks like every rental unit in the development.

I led a divorce workshop in which participants made collages. One man's collage pictured "life as it used to be"—big beautiful house, nice car, picture-perfect family. That sharply contrasted with the right side of his collage. He had one picture of a man sitting on a double bed with an Irish setter at his feet. "That's me," he said, "before and after." He pointed to the bed and the dog, "This is all I ended up with."

3. "Befriend" your living space. Early in my divorce, my friend Eunice Beane gave me this advice: _surround yourself with lots of light, color, music, good smells_. As a single adult, I have learned the wisdom of her advice.

✎ **Pause a moment and test that idea with your reality. In your living space give an example of how you carry out this concept:**

Lots of light: _____

Lots of colors: _____

Lots of music: (maybe your neighbors "supply" that for you!) _____

_____

Lots of good smells: _____

What one decision could you make at a minimum expenditure of money to add an element of each of these four factors to your domicile? Psychologists long have known how the environment impacts the emotions. Too many divorced people create emotionally unhealthy living environments. Remember that cleanliness impacts a living environment as well. Living in a pigsty is hardly a way to maintain a wholesome lifestyle.

Too many divorced people create emotionally unhealthy living environments.

✎ **Let's take a personal check-up. What items around your household are on "tomorrow's" agenda?**

I NEED TO . . .   REAL REASON FOR DELAYING

1. _____   1. _____
2. _____   2. _____
3. _____   3. _____
4. _____   4. _____

3. Loneliness is epidemic in this country. Lots of people are good at hiding their loneliness. Most people are about as lonely as you are. Loneliness is just part of the human condition, especially in a frantic, mobile society like ours. Remaining lonely always is a choice.

4. Take charge of your life. How about inviting some people over? Don't tell me your house is dirty. You just have too bright light bulbs; get some 15-watt light bulbs—your guests won't see any dirt.

✎ **Look over the following list of activities and respond in the appropriate column.**

	Could Do	Could Not Do	Definitely Could Not Do	Have Tried To Do
Eat alone in public	❑	❑	❑	❑
Go to a movie alone	❑	❑	❑	❑
Go to church alone	❑	❑	❑	❑
Go on vacation alone	❑	❑	❑	❑
Go to child's school event	❑	❑	❑	❑
Go to play/symphony	❑	❑	❑	❑
Go to singles event	❑	❑	❑	❑
Go to art museum	❑	❑	❑	❑
Go to Valentine banquet	❑	❑	❑	❑
Go to office party	❑	❑	❑	❑

Which of the above are you most hesitant to do? _____

Why? _____

I have remembered thy name, O Lord, in the night.

–Psalm 119:55, KJV

Your assignment—should you accept—is to select one of the events in the list, to go as a single adult, and report back to the group.

5. Loneliness does not coexist with praise. One alternative to that "wide-awake at 2 a.m." time is to thank the Lord for the good things He has done. (See the verse appearing at left.) So, the next time you're ready to hit the play button on yet another rendition of "The Poor Me Symphony," reach for a praise tape instead. And be prepared to be ambushed by a moment of grace. We certainly miss the intimacy and companionship of a marriage—that's natural—but we can respond on a level that makes us conquerors over loneliness rather than victims of loneliness.

I suggest a "hit" list as a way to conquer loneliness. The first item on my hit list is scrubbing that vile clear plastic shower liner and cleaning the bathtub. Sometimes, I've been en route to my hit list and felt unlonely immediately. Invite the Lord to join you in this moment of loneliness.

Weekly Work

Write in the margin three times this week's memory verse.

Repeat this affirmation:
I need time to readjust to the new realities in my life, including loneliness.

DAY 4

Today's objective:
I will redefine responsibility in light of my progress toward recovery.

Those who carried materials did their work with one hand and held a weapon in the other.

–Nehemiah 4:17

How this phrase applies to divorce recovery—

_____

_____

_____

Redefining Responsibility

Some of us by our attitudes, words, choices, and feelings only manage to further complicate our divorce and to sabotage or detour our trip to recovery. One of our commitments is to healing, the other is to settling up the score. One commitment is to accepting responsibility, the other to shirking responsibility.

The Old Testament story of Nehemiah's rebuilding of Jerusalem applies to divorce recovery. When he told his Jewish friends about his desire and about "the gracious hand of my God upon me," they responded, "Let us start rebuilding" (Nehemiah 2:18). Through this divorce recovery process you are rebuilding your life, and you are cooperating with others in the process. Sanballat and his gang of hoodlums didn't want Jerusalem rebuilt, so they stirred up a lot of opposition and eventually violence toward the rebuilders. See what Nehemiah 4:17 at left says about what the rebuilders did.

Now how does that verse apply to divorce recovery? Growth and recovery will be one goal, but warding off the enemies of recovery will be another. You will be tempted to settle a score here or there, to wimp out on responsibility, to whine, or set the record straight. Sanballat schemed ways to divert Nehemiah's attention. "Come, let us meet together in one of the villages on the plain of Ono" (6:2). Nehemiah had Sanballat pegged and replied, "I am carrying on a great project and cannot go down. Why should the work stop while I leave it and go down with you?" (v. 3). How does the phrase, "I am carrying on a great work" translate into your experience of divorce recovery? Answer this question in the margin box. You may have answered something like this: _Nehemiah accepted responsibility for leading the work of rebuilding the walls of Jerusalem; he determined that nothing would sabotage his goal._

In this week's work we focus on assuming responsibility in six areas: attitudes, words, actions, feelings, money, and recovery.

1. I am responsible for my ATTITUDE. Our attitudes have a way of showing. In most divorces, people have a difficult time having a good attitude. If you take on the martyr's attitude, or the "get-even" attitude, or even the "innocent victim" attitude, you delay healing.

✎ **When was the last time your ex made you mad? Describe it.**

How did you let your ex know you were mad?

_____

Did this latest incident enhance or setback your recovery?

_____

If you had the incident to do over, would you make the same choices?

_____

Ask yourself this question, "Am I/Did I act responsibly with regard to my ex or the settlement?" ❑ Yes ❑ No

What would I have to do in order to say that I was acting/had acted responsibly with my attitudes?

_____

⟱➡ **Stop and pray, asking God to help you act responsibly with your attitudes.**

2. I am responsible for my WORDS. Some of us have short fuses. Some of our exes have had long experience igniting our fuses. Some of us have long experience of holding our fuses out to be lit. Maybe you've said, "Sticks and stones my break my bones, but words will never hurt me!" But words in a divorce can wound; they become the shrapnel ripping through the soul. In the heat of the battle, words get by our lips, sometimes without ever having been near our brains. Sometimes with almost sadistic glee we have seen the words impact almost like bullets; we have seen an ex wince in pain. In the margin box write some of the wounding things you have said to your ex. Have you asked forgiveness from both your ex and from God for saying them? ❑ Yes ❑ No.

You say, "But you don't know what he/she said to me." That's right, I don't, but God does. James wrote, "no man can tame the tongue." We must test how our words sound and resound in the memories of our children. Sometimes we feel like ducking the issue by apologizing for "my choice of words." Or by insisting, "That's not what I meant . . .." Words always are a choice.

⟱➡ **Stop and pray, asking God to help you choose your words responsibly.**

3. I am responsible for my ACTIONS/CHOICES. One of the toughest tasks in divorce recovery is not to respond to provocation. Nehemiah 6:4 points out that Sanballat could be a downright pest. "Four times," Nehemiah pointed

Wounding things I've said to my ex—

_____

_____

_____

_____

Yes, I could pray for the woman who had desecrated my home. It was a hard-won victory. But in the absolute stillness I heard God whisper, reminding me that she was His child, too, as was the man who had inflicted the agony on both of us.[2]

out, "they sent me the same message, and each time I gave them the same answer." Original broken record approach. Some of our exes know just the buttons to push; they probably were the same buttons that got pushed in arguments while we were married. Some of us need to have our circuits rewired or to take the phone off the hook for a bit.

The woman who had a lot to do with breaking up the marriage of Sara Arlene Thrash called Sara and asked, "How have you managed to remain a lady all these years?" Even in the midst of a messy divorce, Sara chose and rechose to conduct herself with integrity. See the quote at left.

 What would I have to do in order to say that I am acting responsibly with my actions/choices?

_____

 Stop and pray, asking God to help you act responsibly with your choices and actions.

Weekly Work

 Continue to memorize this week's memory verse. In the margin write what this verse means to you as you relate it to how you treat your ex.

➡ **Repeat the affirmation appearing at left.**

I need time to readjust to the new realities in my life, including responsibility, which may have to be redefined.

Today's objective:
I will redefine responsibility on the issues of feelings and recovery.

Redefining Responsibility (Part II)

In yesterday's work we reviewed the need for responsible decisions on attitudes, words, and choices. Today we'll look at our responsibility on the issues of feelings and recovery.

4. You are RESPONSIBLE for your feelings. We are a society that is committed to feelings. Feelings are natural. The question is, *What are we going to do with those feelings?* Sara Arlene Thrash wrote about her feelings this way: "I've nursed, coddled, caressed, and embraced my wound, getting maximum mileage out of it and making myself and others about me miserable. A couple of times when it appeared to be dying a natural death, I administered mouth-to-mouth resuscitation, then wondered why I was batting zero."[4]

These honest words call for some kind of response from us. Below check the statements from Sara's comments that apply to you.
❑ I have nursed my wound.
❑ I have coddled my wound.
❑ I have caressed my wound.
❑ I have embraced my wound.
❑ I have gotten maximum mileage out of it.
❑ I have administered mouth-to-mouth resuscitation.
How recently? _____

Most of us keep the "Poor Me Symphony" in the Key of Pain cued up on our tape decks. Hit the button, and instantly we flood our world with the dirge-like laments of, "Oh, poor me . . ." Ever hear the spiritual, "Nobody knows the trouble I've seen. . ."? That may be the unofficial "national anthem" of the divorced.

✎ **What would you have to do in order to say that you are acting responsibly with your feelings?**

_____

⟱ **Stop and pray, asking God to help you act responsibly with your feelings.**

5. You are RESPONSIBLE for your recovery. Some of us know the answers; we just can't apply them to our lives. We've heard the lectures, viewed the videos, read the books, listened to the tapes, filled out the workbooks, and still we're stuck somewhere far short of the finish line. We're like the children of Israel wandering in the desert and longing for our Egypt. Read the verse appearing in the margin about how the Jews complained.

In most of our situations, we cannot go back. That marriage is dead, past tense. Life post-divorce may be a desert, but it still is life, and we can find beauty in the desert.

Maxie Dunnam pointed out the impact of a Jules Feiffer cartoon. The cartoon portrays a husband and wife, staring at each other, bored. The man asks his wife, "Do you believe in life after death?" The woman continues to gaze blankly at her magazine. But she does answer, and her answer is more profound than is the question. "What do you call this?" she asks. [4]

What do you call this period after marriage? Paraphrasing words of Dunnam, I wonder, are you "enduring life, rather than living it"?[5]

⟱ **Read Jesus' words appearing in the margin at left. Do you see any asterisk that excludes people recovering from the pain of divorce? Read His words this way, aloud: "I have come that divorced people may have life, and have it to the full." Read it one more way, aloud: "I have come that (insert your name) may have life, and have it to the full."**

In the verse appearing at left, read how Jesus explained His ministry. Freedom. Recovery. Release—all gifts possible through Jesus. They are gifts with your name on the tags—and when you commit yourself to hearing and doing the work of recovery through the leadership of the Holy Spirit.

✎ **What would I have to do in order to say that I am acting responsibly with the recovery process?**

_____

⟱ **Stop and pray, asking God to help you act responsibly with your recovery process.**

We can trust in God Who moves us toward physical, mental, emotional, and spiritual healing and into the abundant life that Jesus calls us all to.

It would have been better for us to serve the Egyptians than to die in the desert!
—Exodus 14:12

I have come that they may have life, and have it to the full.
—John 10:10

The Spirit of the Lord is on me, because he has anointed me to preach good news to the poor. He has sent me to proclaim freedom for the prisoners and recovery of sight for the blind, to release the oppressed, to proclaim the year of the Lord's favor.
Luke 4:18,19

You may have acted irresponsibly in the past. In dealing with your divorce. you may have made some unwise choices and lived your life in a way that dishonored God. You now may feel that you have treated your ex harshly, or you may feel you have not worked diligently enough at putting the marriage back together. You may feel that you are in prison because of wrongs you've committed. Part of hope and healing of divorce recovery is to allow God to cleanse you from sin.

You can trust Christ's death to pay for your sin. In Acts 16:31, Luke wrote, "Believe in the Lord Jesus, and you will be saved." If you have not done so already, you can receive Jesus Christ right now. If you desire to trust Christ and accept His payment for your sins, tell that to God in prayer right now. You may use this sample prayer to express your faith.

> *Lord Jesus, I need you. I want You to be my Savior and my Lord. I accept Your death on the cross as payment for my sins, and I now entrust my life to Your care. Thank You for forgiving me and for giving me a new life. Please help me grow in my understanding of Your love and power so that my life will bring glory and honor to You. Amen.*

_____ (signature) _____(date)

Trusting in Christ does not guarantee that you will be delivered instantly from problems in life. It does not mean that instantly you will be free from the pain of your divorce. It means that you are forgiven, that you are restored to a relationship with Him that will last throughout eternity, and that you will receive His unconditional love and acceptance, as well as His strength, power, and wisdom, as you continue to grow in your divorce recovery.

I need time to readjust to the new realities in my life, including responsibility for my feelings and for my recovery.

Weekly Work

➠ **Repeat the affirmation appearing at left.**

Notes

[1]Joseph M. Scriven. "What A Friend We Have in Jesus." *The Baptist Hymnal*, (Nashville: Convention Press, 1991), 182.

[2]Sara Arlene Thrash, *Dear God, I'm Divorced*, (Grand Rapids: Baker Book House Company, 1991), 57.

[3]Ibid., 42.

[4]Maxie Dunnam, *The Workbook on Christians Under Construction and In Recovery*, (Nashville: Upper Room Books, 1993), 33.

[5]Ibid., 50.

Resisting Discount Relationships

This week's agenda:
You will choose to resist counterfeit/discount relationships.

A HEALTHY OUTLOOK

Lyla told this story: "It is sad that Mel and I could not share the richness of our marriage until 'death us do part.' But my life did not end with the break-up of our marriage. It is still filled with fun, growth, beauty, joy, and much affection.

"Many supportive and interesting friends enrich my life. I even started my second career at age forty-seven, and today have the best job in the world . . .."[1]

What had Lyla learned about how to view her future? In this chapter we'll discuss how to deal with new relationships.

What you'll learn

This week you will—
- confront the big threats to divorce recovery;
- learn to recognize counterfeit relationships;
- understand how premature relationships abuse divorced people;
- learn to recognize the games of initiating new relationships;
- learn to nurture your relationship potential.

What you'll study

Confronting the Big Threats	Counterfeit Relationships	Premature Relationships	Building Healthy Friendships	Your Relationship Potential
DAY 1	DAY 2	DAY 3	DAY 4	DAY 5

Memory verse

This week's verse of Scripture to memorize—

His divine power has given us everything we need for life and godliness through our knowledge of him who called us by his own glory and goodness.

—2 Peter 1:3

DAY 1

Today's objective:
I will confront the big threats to
healthy divorce recovery.

Confronting the Big Threats

Moments come. Moments go. Divorced individuals can be so wrapped up in
surviving or revenging that they miss the moment to make healthy decisions
which encourage recovery.

Now is a good time to get serious about your commitment to divorce
recovery. You have been in this program for five weeks, but have you made a
real commitment to these agenda decisions and for healthy recovery from
your divorce?

The big threats to healthy recovery at times are camouflaged. You will not
always make clear-cut decisions. Sometimes various shades of gray complicate
decision making. Read more about these four threats.

THREAT #1. THE HEX. Often divorced people wish evil/suffering—or some
of its softer synonyms—on their ex, her/his lawyer, and perhaps on the "other
party." They make comments such as:
• "I hope he gets what's coming to him!"
• "Someday, pal . . . you'll get yours!"
• "God will get you for what you've done . . .."

Because of the hurt, the pain, the confusion, people can say awful things about
those they once loved and may, in fact, still love. Some do not put a hex into
words but nevertheless wish their ex to encounter grief or distress.

Hexes require trips back to the court (and more money to the lawyers) for
restraining orders, peace bonds, and refinement of visitation privileges.
Generally, this only heightens the gamesmanship between exes. Each is
determined to return the volley across the net and to up the stakes. Sadly,
some enlist children, in-laws, friends, and church members in the battles.

Kim's story

Kim told this story about her ex: "He and that woman took away everything
we had worked so hard to get. We had a beautiful home and cars, we traveled,
the kids were in private schools, and now it's all gone. All because of her! I
never really had a chance. His mind was already made up. The last time I saw
him, I told him, 'I hope you burn in hell!' and I meant that. It just burns my
hide to know he's off living it up with that blonde bimbo and here I am stuck
in this dump, trying to make ends meet and living from week to week."

✎ **From your experience with recovery, if you could sit down over coffee
with Kim, what would you say to her?**

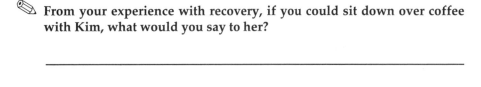

_____

_____

One person answered this way: *I'd try to help Kim understand that she needs to
take care of her own needs rather than spending time and emotional energy stewing
over a situation she can't change—the situation that exists between her ex and the
new woman in his life. I'd suggest that Kim realize that she can harm her physical and
mental health with such a preoccupation.*

I have seen many divorced people who have a life-long regret for words, for anger, for threats, for acts of violence against an ex. We ignore the wisdom in the children's chorus, "Oh, be careful little lips what you say . . .." Words can lacerate, and some words, even though forgiven, are not easily forgotten.

THREAT #2. THE EX. Your ex cannot be neatly incised out of your life, heart, mind, or your life stories, particularly if you have children.

 In a word or phrase describe your relationship with your ex–

during marriage _____

at time of divorce _____

just after divorce _____

currently _____

hopefully in the future _____

Taking responsibility

In the last category, "hopefully in the future," what would you have to do for that hope to become reality? Since we have talked about taking responsibility, what can you do to improve the relationship, even if your ex does nothing?

_____

While we cannot have an ideal relationship with our ex, we can work to create a healthy relationship with appropriate boundaries.

Some of us allow an ex to control, to define, to impact our lives; we still are powerless to defend ourselves. All it takes is one phone call, and all the wounds are reopened. We allow an ex to influence our lives, our hearts, and even our futures. While we cannot have an ideal relationship with our ex, we can work to create a healthy relationship with appropriate boundaries.

Consider Lyla's example: "It is sad that Mel and I could not share the richness of our marriage until 'death us do part.' But my life did not end with the breakup of our marriage. It is still filled with fun, growth, beauty, joy, and much affection. Many supportive and interesting friends enrich my life. I even started my second career at age forty-seven, and today have the best job in the world . . .."[2]

 Reread Lyla's words and underline the key phrase, "My life did not end with the breakup of our marriage." Can you say that?
❑ Yes ❑ No ❑ Unsure

A divorce gives you custody of yourself. What will you do with "yourself"?

If you cannot say that, whose decision is it: yours or your ex's? Lyla did not want a divorce, but a divorce happened. Her ex does not define her life now, post-divorce. Does yours?

 Go back to Lyla's story. Underline the words that describe what her life is filled with. You probably underlined *fun, growth, beauty, joy* and *much affection.* Is your life filled with these things? ❑ Yes ❑ No

If fun, growth, beauty, joy and much affection are not filling your life, where do you begin to make space for such benefits?
1. By _____
2. By _____

*God, grant me
the serenity to accept
the things I cannot
change,
the courage to change
the things I can,
and the wisdom to know
the difference.*[3]

THREAT #3: NO FLEX! As I I walked across a bridge that spans the Tennessee River, I discovered narrow gaps in the bridge that allow expansion/contraction based on heat/cold. Thick steel plates that slide bridge the gaps. As with the bridge, flexibility is essential in surviving divorce. Life has run over you, but you can bounce back! The Serenity Prayer appearing in the margin makes sense to many divorced people.

 What would happen if you genuinely prayed that prayer today?

_____

_____

One person answered the question this way: *If I prayed that prayer, I would take charge of the things about my divorce that were within my power and would put the rest in God's hands.*

THREAT #4: SEX. Sex is a great pain killer; it may be one of the great anesthetics in our contemporary culture. Sex is the way many married couples say, "I'm sorry." Sex and make up. But, sex can be destructive because it distracts from the recovery issues. Some people during separation and even after the divorce still have sex with their exes. Some people assume if the ex wants to have sex, he/she still loves me. That might be true. But it simply might mean that the ex is sexually needy, and the sexual habit with you is established. Your sexual habit and your history get in the way of real healing.

Others dive headfirst into the "swinging-single" scene. Their sexual choices are anger-based sex: "I'll show him/her! Two can play that game." Some choices are need-based: *I need someone to love me, to tell me I'm attractive, I'm desirable, or I'm* (fill in the blank). Sex, when used outside of the good, safe boundaries that God established through marriage, is destructive. Sex outside God's good design can scald and scar and vastly complicate our lives, prolong our pain, and delay our recovery.

So there we have the quartet of factors: the hex, the ex, no flex, and sex. In response to them, we can study our wonderful memory verse for the week "His divine power has given us everything—EVERYTHING—we need [not necessarily what we think we need] for life." We may think, *Oh, I need a mate, I need sex, I need . . .*(fill in the blank). For recovery—for thorough, lasting recovery—I need God. I can trust God to supply what He thinks I need.

For recovery—for thorough, lasting recovery—I need God.

We can remember these truths:
1. I am of value to God and God accepts me through His Son.
2. Others may abandon me or hurt me—but God never will abandon those who put their trust in Him.
3. Life may be tough, but God can help me deal with any reality. God and I are a majority.

Weekly Work

➠ **Say three times this week's memory verse, 2 Peter 1:3.**

➠ **Repeat the statement appearing at left.**

We find no shortage of invitations to the moral "bargain basements."

Counterfeit Relationships

We all love bargains. One major chain advertises, "If you paid full price, you didn't buy it here." A sign that says, "No one beats our low, low prices!" attracts customers. We like bargains, and we like to show off bargains. Unfortunately, we have become a bargain-seeking public where relationships are concerned. We ask ourselves, What's the least I have to invest?

Closely related to the bargain is the counterfeit. *Merriam-Webster's Ninth New Collegiate Dictionary* defines *counterfeit* as *made in imitation of something else with intent to deceive.* Another definition is *to make a fraudulent replica of.*[4] The counterfeit often is of an item that has value or is valued.

One of the big threats to wholesome recovery is a counterfeit or discount relationship. Beverly Raphael has identified seven discount relationship patterns which we will explore here.[5]

1. FANTASY RELATIONSHIPS. In this relationship, you may overlook a lot of warning signals because you so desperately want or need a relationship. You even may be in a race with your ex to see who can get to the altar first for another marriage. (Agenda 9, "Some Biblical Dimensions," discusses the biblical perspective on divorce and remarriage.) People often say:
• He/she is "perfect."
• He/she will never leave me, like my ex did.
• He/she will always love me.
• This is real love.

My friend, Frank Freed, asks counselees who report being "in love" a question that I think should be tattooed on every divorced person's eyelids: *What are you pretending not to know?*

One party fast-forwards the relationship through fantasy. Thus a person is not asking, "What would this person be like to get to know?" but rather, "What would this person be like to be married to?" Moreover, the questioner is not considering realistic answers and, in fact, may be ignoring any data that "douses" the romantic enthusiasm. If you want a fantasy that won't hurt you, try a theme park.

 If you are involved in a relationship with a member of the opposite sex, what might you be pretending not to know? Describe below.

_____

_____

2. REPLACEMENT RELATIONSHIPS. Rather than giving time to grieve the divorce, one or both parties rush into a new relationship to replace the departed spouse. Some look at spouses like carburetors. If someone is having trouble, he or she pulls into a service station and says, "Either fix this one or put a new one in." In the age of the "disposable," we have disposable marital partners or postmarital dating relationships. That is why a person often marries an alcoholic after being divorced from a first alcoholic. Either symbolically or unconsciously, we make the same mistake again.

Today's objective:
I will learn to recognize counterfeit relationships.

Healthy relationships are hard to build and easy to destroy.[6]

The only similarity between fantasy and reality is that they both are seven-letter words which end in y.

3. SELF-DESTRUCTIVE RELATIONSHIPS. If a person feels guilty about a previous relationship, he or she often will make self-destructive choices. Sadly, some people conclude: *I do not deserve the best. Better cut the best deal I can.* Some people volunteer to be victims. If I have not come to terms with what really happened in a marriage and faced it, I will have difficulty making healthy relational choices until I deal with it. Some of us set out to finish the destructive process an ex initiated.

4. AVOIDANT RELATIONSHIPS. Avoiders sidestep any intimacy. Their relationships are brief, transient, and undesirable. While a strong sexual attraction may fuel the relationship, one party realizes that little marriage potential exists. Some people deliberately avoid "nice" men/women. Others hang little "Do Not Disturb" signs over their hearts. Why even go through the details of a relationship? Because, like the song says, "Everybody needs somebody, sometime." "Somebody" generally means any body. Any body will do for people caught up in this pattern of relationship. As soon as anyone drops any hint of "commitment," this party is looking for the nearest exit.

5. COMPULSIVE CAREGIVING RELATIONSHIPS. Some of us are skilled in being rescuers; we rush in to rescue someone from post-divorce trauma. "I know what you are going through. I know what you need: ME!" this person reasons. I call these individuals "emergency-room attendants." Your vital signs aren't looking good, so this person works feverishly to save your life emotionally. He or she assumes that you will be grateful. If I had one piece of advice to offer the newly divorced, it would be: "guard your heart!"

✎ **Think a moment before answering. Have you encountered an E.R.A. (emergency-room attendant) ❏ Yes   ❏ No? Have you acted as an E.R.A.? ❏ Yes   ❏ No**

Many compulsive caregivers reason, "When this is all over, he/she will rise up, recognize my contribution to his or her recovery, and will call me 'blessed.' " This syndrome equally traps males and females; it worms its way into hearts as well as homes.

People initially may welcome such "care"; however, the compulsive caregiver has to be needed and has to keep the care recipient needy. As the treatee gets well, the caregiver starts looking for a more needy person. These so-called "adult" relationships sometimes resemble the concerned mother kissing the skinned knee of a three-year-old. We eventually realize that we are not dating an adult but a father/mother figure.

In most cases, life after divorce will not get better through an outsider's intervention but rather when we commit ourselves to the diligent work of recovery. We can, if needy, be seduced—and not just sexually—into inappropriate relationships—relationships that have no healthy future. What does Proverbs 7:21-22, "With persuasive words she led him astray; she seduced him with her smooth talk. All at once he followed her like an ox going to the slaughter," say about such relationships? Answer at left.

✎ **Have you been seduced emotionally with persuasive words? Yes ❏ No ❏**

What was the end result of that experience? More or less pain?

The primary by-product of involvement with an overly compulsive caregiver is, unfortunately, not wellness but more pain.

How does Proverbs 7:21-22 warn about harmful relationships?

_____

_____

_____

_____

_____

6. POWER AND AGGRESSION RELATIONSHIPS. Who's in charge in your relationships? Some people simply discard all responsibility and "float" through the early days of a divorce. Someone may step in, declare the emotional equivalent of "marital law," and bring stability and security to your world. This can lead to a power struggle with your children (if the "new" person wants to "straighten out" your kids and with your ex and friends as well.) Some single parents are so exhausted by all the responsibilities, they at first welcome the assistance even when the discipline becomes heavy-handed. Assistance generally has strings.

Some recently divorced people turn their lives over to the person they are dating. Ultimately, a tug of war erupts between your ex and the new man/woman in your relationship. You get caught between your ex and your "current." Eventually, you may feel that you need another divorce—this time, from a relationship. Sadly many cannot easily remove themselves. We even may ignore our own inner wisdom to take advice from a new romantic flame.

7. SAME OLD PROBLEM/FRESH FACE. The first months of a discount relationship can be exiting: someone cares about you, compliments you, takes you places, makes you feel alive, offers you kernels of hope. But eventually the old problems/habits surface. Read 1 Peter 5:8 appearing at left. The New Testament is clear that we have an enemy who, as Peter knew from personal experience, can sneak up on us. What would you say the devil's task is in the midst of your divorce? Or at this present time? Write your answer at left.

One person answered the question this way: *The devil's task in my divorce is to keep me looking for someone—even if it's just anyone—who will show me a good time because I'm afraid of being lonely.*

You safely can conclude the devil will not encourage you to work on recovery issues. For some people, the enemy may use drugs or alcohol to dull our pain; for others he will use a sexual relationship. The enemy keeps tabs on our weaknesses and our vulnerabilities. He knows which would be easy areas of conquest. The devil will try to "pass off" something relationally that may not be the best for you. The question is: will you buy it?

Weekly Work

✎ **In the margin write this week's memory verse.**

Premature Relationships

Ever get a small pebble in your shoe? At first you may try to ignore it, but eventually you must stop and shake out the pebble. Amazing how a small pebble can create such discomfort!

What will sidetrack you from your pilgrimage to recovery? Perhaps what sidetracks you is not some gigantic boulder; perhaps a small "pebble" of a premature relationship will be enough to derail you.

In yesterday's work we studied discount and counterfeit relationships. In this section, we will study premature relationships—relationships for which you

---

Be self-controlled and alert. Your enemy the devil prowls around like a roaring lion looking for someone to devour.

–1 Peter 5:8

The devil's task—

_____

_____

_____

_____

DAY 3

Today's objective:
I will understand how premature relationships abuse divorced people.

are not ready. I have found that healthy people grieve and unhealthy people replace. Emotionally and spiritually unhealthy people replace the ex. Sometimes they act with lightning speed and even with overlapping relationships. They say "yes" to relationships long before they have finished the work of the loss.

Divorced people frequently ask, "How long before I get over this?" Without flinching, I say two to four years. People have moaned, groaned, cursed, and questioned my sanity when they hear my answer. They reply, "But, but, I want to be over it NOW!" But replacement will lead you to a bad relationship in most cases and possibly to another divorce.

1. PREMATURE RELATIONSHIPS ABUSE BY CIRCUMVENTING HEALING. Fast healing is not always a possibility. Some workaholics who race back to work prematurely after major surgery suffer a relapse. The same thing occurs with divorce recovery. No instant one-two-three's.

To begin a relationship before adequate time has elapsed may mean you are too close to the experience to interpret it accurately. So, to make yourself look/sound good to this new flame, you may "tiptoe" over some of your contribution to the divorce. Thus, we are tempted to blame everything on the "ex." Initially, some of us are not good at owning up to our contribution, even if it was small. Recovery requires that we face our own involvement in the demise of a marriage.

Many times, in early dating, you can drift into a "My ex was a bigger rat than your ex!" mentality. Saying this clearly indicates that your ex still is involved in your life and is sabotaging your healing.

> ✎ **In the three paragraphs you just read, underline words or phrases that call attention to the dangers of a premature relationship.**

You may have underlined such phrases as *too close to the experience, tiptoe over your contribution, blame everything on the ex, drifting into a "My ex was a bigger rat than your ex!" mentality.* All these clearly show how we can sabotage recovery.

2. PREMATURE RELATIONSHIPS ABUSE BY DIVERTING ATTENTION FROM THE RECOVERY PROCESS. We all need time to heal. Premature relationships keep us from allotting generous amounts of time to heal—to have the stitches out before we begin dating. We schedule everything else; why not schedule ample time for the recovery process?

Recovery is difficult work. You are giving lots of time to this divorce-recovery process. To be part of this group involved in divorce recovery you have been willing to say: *I am investing in my future.* Why not really invest in your future and set a moratorium on dating?

You'd probably prefer to skip some of these assignments. When they begin to work on a certain topic, some people play games and say, "Oh, I don't have any problems with that." But one of the biggest threats to recovery is denial.

3. PREMATURE RELATIONSHIPS ABUSE BY HAMSTRINGING THE FUTURE. One of the movements of the "Poor Me Symphony" is the notion: *I'll never marry again.* Just because I do not have someone in my life at the moment does not mean I won't in the future. In giving myself adequate time

Recovery is an investment— the high road. Replacement is immediate— the low road.

You have plenty of time to rebuild and to heal. You are not ready for the future until you have finished with the business of the past. Time is one luxury that you can afford during this period.

to heal, I well may be in the right place and the right shape at the right time when the right one comes along.

 Below is author Steve Arterburn's "Progression of a Healthy Relationship," with the stages listed in the incorrect order. Number them in the order in which you believe someone establishes a healthy relationship. The answers appear on page 83. [7]

PROGRESSION OF A HEALTHY RELATIONSHIP

_6_ Sacrifice _5_
_7_ Giving of self _4_
_12_ Sexual intimacy _11_
_2_ Mutual interest
_1_ Attraction
_5_ Discernment of God's will _8_
_11_ Marriage _10_
_9_ Love _6_
_()_ Ripening maturity
_8_ Intimacy _7_
_4_ Deepening trust _12_
_3_ Enjoyment
_10_ Commitment _9_

We always are tempted to get the cart before the horse. People committed to recovery insist on first things first, even when doing so is inconvenient.

My friend Mike Murdock has come up with some wonderful questions—I call them "zappers"—to help us evaluate healthy relationships.
Zapper 1: What initiated your initial relationship?
Zapper 2: Does the conversation that excites you produce joy in him/her?
Zapper 3: Does your relationship balance seriousness and fun?
Zapper 4: Does he/she appreciate your friends?
Zapper 5: Are you as excited to be with him/her in public as in private?
Zapper 6: Is his/her interest in growth compatible with yours?
Zapper 7: Does he/she release or mute your energy?
Zapper 8: Do you really know enough about him/her?
Zapper 9: Is satisfying your sexual desires and relational desires the real reason for being in this relationship at this time?[8]

A premature relationship may set our recovery back, may delay our healing, and may give us fresh wounds that need healing. Thus, we will not be in a healthy place when the right one comes along.

In too many instances the premature relationship leads to a premature or outright unhealthy marriage which leads eventually to divorce number two.

I will save myself some scars by saying "no" to premature relationships. I will give myself time to heal thoroughly.

Weekly Work

 In the margin write in your own words this week's memory verse.

➡ **Repeat the affirmation that appears at left.**

DAY 4

Today's objective:
I will learn as a divorced person how to build healthy friendships.

"He never talks to me."

Building Healthy Friendships

We are not designed to be Lone Rangers; even the "Masked Man" had his faithful sidekick, Tonto. Friends, old and new, can help foster healing and recovery. Early in the divorce process you learned who your "real" friends were. You may want to turn back to page 42 and review the material on friendships you have lost and gained through or as a result of the divorce.

Friendships are essential for survival and thrival during post-divorce. But many divorced people were so couple-oriented that they as single adults do not know how to initiate, build, or nurture healthy adult relationships. The healthiest friendships are two-way; friendships thrive when both friends value and nurture the friendship. Here are some elements of a healthy friendship:

1. Everyday life. Like a quilt, our strongest friendships are composed of bits and pieces of everyday life. Day in, day out, over time, we become friends. We see a friend through all kinds of situations; that is why we feel pain when a friend moves away—either geographically or emotionally. When you don't have a spouse, the friend is the first person to hear the good and the bad news.

2. Dialogue. Some people believe that men have fewer dialogue skills than women do and as a result have fewer friendships. They believe that men rarely talk about themselves and talk only about sports and work. Some people argue that males have friendships based on doing (hunting or fishing, watching basketball, working on cars, their work), while females have friendships based on being. How many counselors have heard the complaint, "He never talks to me," to which the man retorts, "What is there to say?" Sometimes a husband is talkative while his wife is the silent partner. Couples that spent hours before marriage talking find that post-marriage they have little to talk about, other than the kids. When the kids are grown, what do you have to talk about at breakfast? "Catching up" is one of the major pastimes between friends.

3. Affirmation. A friend accepts unconditionally. He/she accepts me as I am. This becomes extremely important for the individual who has been rejected through divorce; friends become the cheerleaders on the sideline. Edna told this story: "By the time he and his lawyer got through with me, I didn't have a shred of self-esteem left. But my friend Kim stood with me. I called her, many a night, at midnight. Sometimes she would just call and say, 'I'll pick you up in ten minutes. You need to get out of that house.'"

✎ **Do you have one friend who really has affirmed you? If so, identify the friend and describe how that person affirmed you. If not, ask God to put this type of friend in your path.**

My friend _____ really affirmed me by _____

_____

Have you ever thanked your friend? In the margin box identify ways you could express your thanks.

Ways to say thanks—

_____

_____

_____

_____

4. Trust. "I can tell him/her things and they never will go any further." In fact, one of the worst betrayals, after the loss of a spouse in a divorce, occurs when a friend cannot keep confidences.

5. Time. I do not believe in instant friendships. Why? Because most of us do not make good/strong first impressions; only over time do our real qualities shine. Real friendships take time. That's why people who haven't seen each other in years can get together and take up where they last left off: the time spent previously is a solid foundation.

6. Be There. As one popular song says, "All you have to do is call . . . and I'll be there." A friend comes through. One of the greatest friendships in the Bible is that between a shepherd, David, and King Saul's heir apparent, Jonathan. The friendship—technically they were brothers-in-law—was challenged because Saul kept trying to kill David; often Jonathan warned David about ways to escape. In the twenty-third chapter of 1 Samuel, David is on the run for his life. He desperately needs a friend. See the verse appearing at left.

✎ **Below name the friend or friends who in your divorce process have helped you find strength in God.**

_____

_____

In the margin box describe a particular incident in which this person or these people helped you find strength in God.

Divorce offers two new realities. First, it is a chance to build solo rather than duo friendships. Have you ever met someone that your spouse clearly did not like and did not want you to like? Maybe you met someone, but his or her spouse drove you crazy. Couples generally socialize with other couples. Now, your spouse doesn't have "veto" power over new friendships. At times, some friendships become clouded because one friend wants more and either the other does not recognize that desire or does not want that as a goal, or not as a goal at the moment—perhaps in time. The issue often comes to a head when one friend starts seriously dating another person.

Sometimes casual friendships do lead to marriage. How can a person keep up the "safe" boundaries if both do not desire marriage to come out of the friendship? Andy Bustanoby has given the following insight for distinguishing between a non-romantic friendship and a romantic friendship:

FRIENDSHIP
- Focus on mutual interests.
- Spend a great deal of time together.
- Drawn by mutual interests.
- Doesn't think about marriage to this friend.
- Focus is on how the friendship is mutually beneficial.
- Treats person as brother/sister.

ROMANTIC FRIENDSHIP
- Focus on each other.
- When spending time together resent intrusion of a third party.

And Saul's son Jonathan went to David at Horesh and helped him find strength in God.

–1 Samuel 23:16

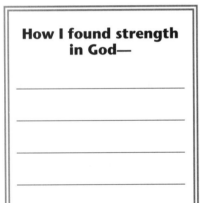

How I found strength in God—

_____

_____

_____

_____

To resist counterfeit, discount, and premature relationships, invest in solid friendships.

- Driven to the person by unspoken needs for emotional support and affirmation.
- Spends time fantasizing about being married to this person.
- Focus is on how the friendship benefits you rather than him/her.
- Cannot treat person as merely a brother/sister.[9]

For successful divorce recovery you need a cadre of friends, male and female, who are there and will be there for you. That prolific author named Anonymous observed, "A friend is someone who walks in when the world walks out."

I will give myself time to heal by investing in good friendships.

Weekly Work

 **In the margin write what this week's memory verse means to you.**

➠ **Repeat the affirmation appearing in the margin.**

Your Relationship Potential

DAY 5

Today's objective:
I will nurture my relationship potential.

"Say YES! to the best!" That's a line I write in many books before I autograph them. It's a wonderful way to live—saying yes to the best/saying no to the discount, the counterfeit, the premature, the "less-than-the-best." We base saying "YES" to the best on these spiritual underpinnings or foundations.

1. WE NURTURE OUR ROMANTIC/RELATIONAL POTENTIAL BY TRUSTING GOD. Joseph Girzone said: "I made up my mind that I was not going to forge my own way through life but instead would let God guide me. And it makes good sense. God didn't create us haphazardly. He made each of us for a purpose and He is determined that we accomplish that purpose. He does, however, need our cooperation, and when we give Him our goodwill and open our hearts to Him (which is really all we have to offer), He sets in motion all the machinery we need to fulfill the task He has planned for us."[10]

Girzone used the phrase "made up my mind." "Made up my mind" is active: *I have decided*, rather than passive: *It has been decided for me*.

 **Go back and underline the two decisions Girzone made.**

I have made up my mind about—

_____

_____

_____

_____

You likely underlined *I was not going to forge my own way through life* and *I would let God guide me*. In the margin box write some things you have made up *your* mind about. Did you write something like, *I have made up my mind that my ex will pay for all the unhappiness he has caused me!* or something like, *I have made up my mind that I am going to get over this divorce*? How do your decisions match up with Girzone's?

 **What would you have to give up in order to let God actively guide you?**

_____

➠ **Stop and pray, asking God to help you let Him guide you.**

2. WE NURTURE OUR ROMANTIC/RELATIONAL POTENTIAL BY SAYING "NO" AND SAYING IT OFTEN. Many divorced people look in a new relationship for someone better than the ex. The ex becomes the yardstick against which we compare all. The past determines the future. That is why getting into romantic relationships so soon after a divorce, before the heart has healed thoroughly and before you have changed your orientation from past tense to future tense and have studied the biblical guidelines if you are contemplating possible remarriage, defeats the recovery process.

✎ **Do you remember the discussion of premature relationships in day 3? Based on what you learned in that discussion, write the missing words in the sentence below.**

Emotionally healthy and spiritually healthy people _____ the divorce. Emotionally and spiritually unhealthy people _____ the ex.

You likely wrote *grieve* and *replace* in the blanks. In what ways have you been anxious to replace rather than grieve? In the margin box write your answer.

We will have invitations to the bargain basement or perhaps to "compromise city" that occur as part of the romantic rebuilding after a divorce. God's grace can help us decline those invitations.

3. WE NURTURE OUR ROMANTIC/RELATIONAL POTENTIAL BY KNOWING WHAT WE DO NOT WANT AND WHAT WE DO WANT. You have the chance to be wiser because of your experience and to learn lessons that you only can learn through this pain. But will you learn? You need time to think about what qualities you value, what qualities you cannot appreciate, what you want, and what you definitely do not want.

This also is a time for God to remold some of your wants—a time to hear God's voice and to become aware of God's will for your life and God's commitment to the best. Fill in the margin box as it applies to your relationships.

4. WE NURTURE OUR ROMANTIC/RELATIONAL POTENTIAL BY WAITING WELL. People don't want to wait well. They want things now. How many divorced people suffer from the "poverty of impatience"? God will bring "the machinery" into your life, but it will be on His timetable. Whether we wait for a season of romance, for a right relationship, for a relationship or friendship with a future, we can wait well.
Here are some tips on waiting—
1. Keep your eyes on Jesus.
2. Live in the present, not the future, or the past.
3. Release control daily. Let go.
4. Don't try to "help" God.
5. Remember: Closed doors are God's blessings.[10]

5. WE NURTURE OUR ROMANTIC/RELATIONAL POTENTIAL BY DEVELOPING THE ABILITY TO DISTINGUISH BETWEEN HEALTHY AND UNHEALTHY RELATIONSHIPS. Some of us have been in so many dysfunctional second-rate relationships, we have negated our ability to distinguish between what is healthy and what is unhealthy. Steve Arterburn has offered a wonderful profile to contrast the healthy with the unhealthy. This profile appears on the next page.

How I've been anxious to replace rather than grieve—

_____

_____

_____

_____

Qualities I looked for the first time—

_____

_____

_____

Qualities God wants me to look for—

_____

_____

_____

HEALTHY RELATIONSHIPS	UNHEALTHY RELATIONSHIPS
Reality-based	Fantasy-based
Completes another	Seeks to be completed
Finds a friend	Seeks a victim
Sacrifices	Demands sacrifice
Patient	Impatient
Kind	Rude
Forgiving	Resentful
Doesn't hold grudges	Seeks revenge
Born out of security	Born out of fear
Vulnerable	Defensive
Allowed to develop	Pressed to perform
Honest	Deceitful[12]

✎ **In the chart you just read circle the traits that describe your previous marriage. Underline once those that describe your last relationship. Underline twice those that describe your current relationship. Put a star by the ones you need to work on.**

The way to healing is through God and not through relational or romantic ecstasy!

Weekly Work

▥➡ **Repeat the affirmation appearing in the margin.**

I will nurture my relational potential by saying "Yes" to what is best and "No" to anything less than the best.

Notes

[1]Lyla White, "Forward" in _Stranger at the Gate_ by Mel White, (New York: Simon & Schuster, 1994), 6.

[2]Ibid.

[3]Reinhold Niebuhr, "The Serenity Prayer," (St. Meinrad, IN: Abbey Press)

[4]_Webster's Ninth New Collegiate Dictionary_, (Springfield, MA: Merriam-Webster, 1983), 297.

[5]Adapted from Beverly Raphael, _The Anatomy of Bereavement_, (New York: Basic Books, 1983), 219.

[6]From _Addicted to Love_, ©1991 by Stephen Arterburn. Published by Servant Publications, Box 8617, Ann Arbor, Michigan 48107. Used by permission. 261.

[7]Ibid., 255.

[8]Adapted from Michael Murdock presentation, PTL, May 7, 1984.

[9]Andy Bustanoby, "Pushing the Limit," _Christian Single_, April 1994, 21.

[10]Joseph Girzone, _Never Alone: A Personal Way to God_, (New York: Doubleday, 1994), 26-27.

[11]Adapted from Bob Kerner with Sandi Kerner, "Waiting," _Christian Healing Ministry News_, v. 6 (February 1993), 3.

[12]Arterburn, 261.

Here are answers to the exercise you completed on page 78 about the progression of a healthy relationship. The correct order is 1. Attraction, 2. Mutual interest, 3. Enjoyment, 4. Giving of self, 5. Sacrifice, 6. Love, 7. Intimacy, 8. Discernment of God's will, 9. Commitment, 10. Marriage, 11. Sexual intimacy, 12. Deepening trust, 13. Ripening maturity.

AGENDA
6

This week's agenda:
You will redeem the process and accept resurrection.

Accepting Resurrection

WHEN A FUTURE SEEMED DIM

Kathy's husband ran off with Kathy's best friend. He filed for divorce. He and the new woman in his life married two days after the divorce was final. For the next two years Kathy was in and out of hospitals dealing with gastrointestinal difficulties that doctors said were related to stress. Because of repeated absences for illness, Kathy lost her job.

To learn to cope with the difficulties in her life, Kathy joined a support group at her church. This was the beginning of a brighter future for Kathy. (Read the story on page 96 about how she turned these tragic events into a time of victory in her life.)

What you'll learn

This week you will—
- learn how God "partners" with the wounded;
- recognize ways we sabotage God's grace;
- explore our futures as divorced individuals;
- understand that resurrection also is a process;
- learn how to accept God's forgiveness.

What you'll study

God Partners with the Broken	Limiting God's Grace	Sabotaging God's Grace	Accepting God's Forgiveness	Knowing Where You Are Going
DAY 1	DAY 2	DAY 3	DAY 4	DAY 5

Memory verse

This week's verse of Scripture to memorize—
And we know that in all things God works for the good of those who love him, who have been called according to his purpose.

—Romans 8:28

DAY 1

Today's objective:
I will learn how God "partners" with the wounded

God Partners with the Broken

Sometimes I think that glue could be a second symbol of the church. God works intricately to restore that which has been broken, marred, scarred and tossed onto the relational junk heap. God is the master craftsman who specializes in restoring broken, wounded people.

1. GOD WEEPS WITH US. Many of us have heard the story of the little boy whose teacher asked him what he was drawing. "God," the little boy answered without hesitation. "God!" the teacher sputtered. "No one knows what God looks like." "They will when I get through," the boy answered confidently. When God gets through working in your life after all the pain of a divorce, some people will say, "So that is what God is like!"

My colleague, Bobbie Reed, conducted doctoral research on how children from single-parent homes understand God. She discovered that those children were not inhibited in portraying a God Who cared. One drawing shows a family at the beach; sure enough, on a towel lies God. The young artist had no problem explaining that God goes with her and her brothers and her mother to the beach or other places so that He can look after them.

If only we adults could have this simple concept of God! We may be as angry (or at least annoyed) at God as we are at our ex. We think God did not come through on our timetable to save our marriage. We become angry at all those joyous stories of people God rescued in the nick of time. *If He saved their marriages, why did He not save mine?* In the margin box describe how you've felt at such times.

God is touched by our pain and by our divorces. After all, He created marriage. He designed it to be so much more than most of us experienced. Jason Towner wrote:

> *Divorce is not God's creation;*
> * he has never pronounced it good.*
> *He did not ordain it for man's welfare;*
> * rather, it exists.*
> *He'd much rather man enjoy the intimacies and love*
> * of a Christian marriage*
> *   than endure the loneliness and hardship*
> *   of a divorce.*
> *But he gave man the power to make decisions;*
> * He trusted man.*
> *The first divorce was not between man and woman*
> * but between man and God.*
> *And the Garden must have been lonely for God*
> * after Adam and Eve were gone.*[1]

2. GOD CARES. The woman loudly recited her woes as a divorced single mother of three. Finally, she stopped, looked at the single-adult minister, and demanded, "Well?" He fumbled for a moment and then said, "Well, God cares." "God cares. Is that the best you can do? How is that going to pay my rent this month?" she queried. God may not pay her rent, but God can place it on someone's heart—if that person obeys—to bring the money into her life or can help her be resourceful to think of ways for additional funding. God will find ways to show us that He cares. When I was a funeral director, I often heard at funerals the song "Does Jesus Care?"

Does Jesus care?

> Does Jesus care when my heart is pained
> Too deeply for mirth and song,
> As the burdens press, and the cares distress,
> And the way grows weary and long?
> Does Jesus care when my way is dark
> With a nameless dread and fear?
> As the daylight fades into deep night shades,
> Does he care enough to be near?
> Does Jesus care when I've tried and failed
> to resist some temptation strong;
> When for my deep grief I find no relief,
> Tho my tears flow all the night long?2

Ever asked those kinds of questions when you lie awake about 4 a.m.? I have, and I suspect the song's author had, too.

 Go back to the song and underline words or phrases with which you identify.

Then, in the concluding lines, the author answers the questions forcefully from personal experience:

> Oh, yes, He cares; I know He cares.
> His heart is touched with my grief.
> When the days are weary, and the long nights dreary,
> I know my Savior cares.³

 Now go back to these four lines and underline the words of promise.

The line that captures my attention is, "His heart is touched with my grief." The heart of God is touched with MY grief. What an amazing thought! On earth Jesus encountered sad, spent, brokenhearted people like the single parent at Nain; he stopped the funeral procession for her only son and "gave" him back to her (Luke 7:15). At the tomb of Lazarus, "Jesus wept" (John 11:35). Even Mary and Martha, sisters of Lazarus, scolded Jesus for His lack of consideration. Read the verse appearing at left to see what they said. Have you ever said something like that to Jesus? You may have said something like, "Lord, if You had cared enough, this divorce never would have happened."

Lord . . . if you have been here, my brother would not have died.

–John 11:21

3. GOD WILL DESIGN WAYS TO LET US KNOW HE CARES. One of my favorite Old Testament verses is 2 Samuel 14:14, which contradicts the cliche, "You can't cry over spilled milk." This verse appears at left.

Like water spilled on the ground which cannot be recovered, so we must die. But God does not take away life, instead he devises ways so that a banished person may not remain estranged from him.

–2 Samuel 14:14

 What comes to mind when you read the word *"devises"*? In the context of this study, what could this passage mean? Below write your answer.

_____

One person answered this way: *In this verse I see God taking an active approach to my life. If He devises ways, it means that He is actively pursuing me and wanting no separation between me and Him.*

The life of gifted song writer Charles Weigle demonstrates this truth—that God does care. Despair came in Weigle's life when his wife took his daughter and left him. In desperation, Charlie Weigle walked the streets of Miami to a long pier over Biscayne Bay. According to his friend, Frank Eifert, "Charles Weigle sat on the pier through the longest night he had ever known," wrestling with the temptation to drop into the dark waters and end it all.

Greater care than that of a friend

A new day dawned. After Good Friday comes Eastern morn. After he watched the sun rise, he stood and walked home. For five years he wrote nothing. Then one afternoon, about sundown, Weigle began reflecting on God's goodness to him which he had seen in his friends who had cared for him during his divorce. Still, he noted, none of them cared for him like Jesus did. Weigle walked to the piano and began writing the words to a new song he called "No One Ever Cared for Me Like Jesus," which spoke of how Jesus changed him completely and took away the sin and darkness in his life.

Sometime later, when Charlie Weigle attended a service in Indianapolis, the great songmaster, Homer Rodeheaver, asked Weigle to sing. "Charlie," he called, "come and sing something for us." That night Charlie Weigle sang for the first time his "No One Ever Cared for Me Like Jesus,"[4] a song that has brought comfort to thousands in all types of distress. Charlie Weigle learned— as you already may have learned—that in the midst of our pain, if we look and listen closely, we will realize that we are not alone. God is present. God does care.

Weekly Work

 Begin to memorize this week's memory verse, **Romans 8:28**. Write it three times in the margin.

Not even this will be able to defeat God's plan and love for me.

▥▶ Repeat the affirmation that appears at left.

<table>
<tr><td>

DAY

2

</td></tr>
</table>

Today's objective:
I will recognize the ways we limit God's grace.

Limiting God's Grace

Have you ever wondered why all those genealogies are in the Bible? So-and-so begat so-and-so—mostly with names we cannot begin to pronounce accurately. Long lists of names. We may wonder why we need to know information like: "A record of the genealogy of Jesus Christ the son of David, the son of Abraham: Abraham was the father of Isaac, Isaac the father of Jacob. Jacob the father of Judah and his brothers." (Matthew 1:1-2).

What good is that information when my ex is denying access to our children? What good is that when my ex is three months behind in alimony? What good is that when my oldest says he wants to go live with his father?

Perhaps you will understand more after we read this powerful case study of forgiveness. In this story, David, the great king of Israel, has done the unthinkable: he has sent his men into the field while he has remained behind in Jerusalem. Second Samuel 11 reports the event, which takes place "in the spring, at the time when kings go off to war" (v. 1).

A powerful case study of forgiveness

One night, King David cannot sleep, so he walks around on the roof of the palace and sees a woman bathing—not just any woman but a very beautiful woman. David asks who she is and is told that her name is Bathsheba and that her husband's name is Uriah. David sends for her, she visits the palace and his bedroom, and they commit adultery; she goes back home. Weeks later, she informs David, "I am pregnant."

Oops. David had not counted on this. So, David quickly thinks and decides to send for Uriah, the husband, who is on the front lines defending this philandering king. Under the guise of gaining some military info, he sends for Uriah. So, the king—after plotting all this out in his mind—says, "Say, I bet you miss your wife—camping out in the fields with your soldier pals. Yeah, why don't you go see her?" David must have prided himself on how easily he duped the guy.

Next morning, an aide visits the king and says that Uriah didn't go home the previous night. In fact, he spent the night on the mats with his master's servants. David sends for the husband/soldier and asks him why he didn't go to his wife. Uriah may have thought that this was some kind of test. "As surely as you live I will not do such an outrageous thing. If my men cannot sleep with their wives, I cannot sleep with mine," Uriah replies.

So David throws a little party and gets Uriah drunk. He must have thought, *If I can get him drunk enough, nine months from now, he'll never suspect a thing.* Next morning, the aide reports that Uriah didn't go home that night either. David has, at best, one uncooperative husband. So he drafts an order to the head of the military, "Put Uriah in the front line where the fighting is fiercest. Then withdraw from him so he will be struck down and die" (2 Samuel 11:15). In an act of cowardice, David has Uriah murdered.

So King David brings Bathsheba to his house and takes her as his wife. *What a compassionate king!* everyone thinks. The Scriptures tell us about David's actions, "But the thing David had done displeased the Lord." Nathan is assigned to confront the king with the charges of adultery and murder. David finally replies, "I have sinned against the Lord."

"And so they all lived happily ever after." Hardly. Here's what happened:
(1) David prayed the great 51st Psalm. Psalm 51:10 reads, "Create in me a pure heart, O God, and renew a steadfast spirit within me."
(2) The baby died.
(3) David comforted Bathsheba and she got pregnant again—this time as David's wife.
(4) They had a son and named him Solomon.

Now, surely we can conclude "and they all lived happily ever after." No, it didn't turn out in storybook fashion. David's family was grand champion of dysfunctionality. Years of devastating pain lay ahead. Bathsheba disappears. We will hear little from her until Matthew's genealogies. Actually, we will not find her name, only her status. Check Matthew 1:6 appearing in the margin for another "slice" of the genealogy.

Jesse [was] the father of King David. David was the father of Solomon, whose mother had been Uriah's wife.
        –Matthew 1:6

 Why do you think the Bible includes those genealogies? Below write your answer.

_____

Does the verse you read at the beginning of this lesson give you a clue? Here it is again: "A record of the genealogy of Jesus Christ the son of David, the son of Abraham: Abraham was the father of Isaac, Isaac the father of Jacob. Jacob the father of Judah and his brothers" (Matthew 1:1-2).

In the verse appearing in the margin on the previous page, do you spot those two words: *had been*? Bathsheba—an adulteress—is front and center in the family tree of Jesus. David—an adulterer and murderer—is front and center in the family tree of Jesus. Why? To illustrate God's great, unfathomable mercy and grace.

God could have killed David/Bathsheba. God could have fired David as king. God could have made them infertile. God could have done all of these things. Yet, God did not act as we would expect. He chose to offer mercy. God chose to bestow heaps of grace on a king with an overactive libido.

✎ **What is the Word of God for divorced people that underlies the words of this Scripture? What does this passage say to you? What insights have you gained into God's grace?**

_____

_____

_____

Bathsheba and David are in the genealogy to remind us that Jesus did not have a perfect family tree. Bathsheba and David are there to remind us that if God forgave them under the law and gave them a second chance and a son named Solomon—a son God loved—how much more can He forgive us through the mercy of Jesus? Bathsheba and David are there to remind us that God "so loves the world" that He acts—present tense—equally graciously to people today who have sinned in an outrageous way and who turn to Him. God never changes. If you let Him, He will act toward you in an outrageously merciful way. He even may act toward your ex in an outrageously merciful way. How will you react if He does?

God has no junk piles. God is not even thinking about getting in the junkyard business. Indeed, as the hymn says, "There Is A Wideness in God's Mercy." What do you need most this moment? Could it be that you need forgiveness? Or reassurance of forgiveness when you seek it?

➠ **Stop and pray, telling God what you need most and asking Him to grant it to you.**

Weekly Work

➠ **Say aloud three times this week's memory verse.**

➠ **Repeat the affirmation appearing at left. Fill in the blank with whatever applies to you.**

Not even _____ will be able to limit or defeat God's plan and love for me.

DAY

3

Sabotaging God's Grace

Today's objective:
I will recognize the ways divorced people sabotage God's grace.

Forgiveness is an invitation—an invitation many divorced people are reluctant to accept fully. Our memory verse reminds us that "in all things (including divorce) God works for the good of those who love him." One of the ways He works for our good is through granting forgiveness and by inviting us to participate in the forgiveness process.

Forgiveness is, to some degree, letting someone off the hook. That goes against the grain for most divorced people. We want justice, thank you very much.

God has endowed humankind with two Godlike capacities: to reproduce and to forgive. Luke 6:37-38 underscores God's commitment to forgiveness.

- "Do not judge and you will not be judged."
- "Do not condemn and you will not be condemned."
- "Forgive, and you will be forgiven."
- "Give, and it will be given to you."

I wish Scripture said, "Be forgiven and you will forgive." But Jesus implies that we have to take some initiative: You forgive first. That is such difficult work for some of us. Here are some things to remember about forgiveness:

1. SOME DIVORCED PEOPLE THINK FORGIVENESS IS AN EMOTION. "But I don't feel like forgiving my ex!" you might say. But do you really have any right to draw out the forgiveness process? Many people live as if some day a feeling will come over them and lead them to forgive their exes and the third party, the lawyer, or the friends who took the ex's side. Sometimes we have to be bold and go on the forgiveness initiative. Sometimes we have to examine our hearts and ask God to lead us to actively forgive.

Sometimes we have to be bold and go on the forgiveness initiative.

➠ **Stop and pray. Ask God to show you whether you have been living as if you believe forgiveness is a feeling. Ask Him to show you whether you have been postponing the work of forgiveness.**

2. SOME DIVORCED PEOPLE THINK FORGIVENESS DEPENDS ON BEING ASKED FOR FORGIVENESS FIRST. You may say, "Oh, of course, I'll forgive him/her—after all, I have to—but I want him/her to come to me and ask my forgiveness." Did you insert, "to crawl to me?" We often envision our exes asking (begging? pleading?) for forgiveness. But what if he/she never asks forgiveness? You say, "Then I am just not going to forgive until he/she does. And I had better hear a 'pretty please.'" Such an attitude ties you to the past rather than leads you into God's future.

Have you ever said "pretty please" to the Lord? Why then should your ex have to "set up" his/her request for your forgiveness with a "pretty please"?

"Forgive, and you will be forgiven." Not my words, but Jesus' words.

➠ **Stop and pray, asking God to show you whether you have been living as if you believed that forgiveness depends on being asked for forgiveness first.**

3. SOME DIVORCED PEOPLE THINK FORGIVENESS DEPENDS ON SOME MATHEMATICAL FORMULA. Peter asked Jesus, "Lord, how many times shall I forgive my brother when he sins against me? Up to seven times?"

(Matthew 18:21). Peter obviously was trying to suggest an answer to Jesus and also was suggesting "seven" to be pretty generous.

Many of us have long pre-divorce records of forgiving or seeking forgiveness by saying, "Honey, it never will happen again. I promise." Perhaps we believed that it—whatever "it" was—never *would* happen again, but it did. Some of us simply have lost count. In some cases, the "last-straw" time occurred when forgiveness had been so cheapened as to be ineffective. You may ask, "How many times do I have to forgive?" I have no easy answers.

Jesus goes on to say about forgiveness, "I tell you, not seven times, but seventy times seven." Some people would be quick to say: "OK, that's a total of 490 times," and you conclude that your ex already has used up most if not all of the forgiveness bank.

For with the measure you use, it will be measured to you.

–Luke 6:38

Jesus is saying, "Keep forgiving." In the margin read the Scripture about what Jesus says about the mathematics of mercy.

 Below write what that verse means to you.

_____

_____

You could have written something like this: *If I am stingy with forgiveness, God will be stingy with me.*

5. SOME DIVORCED PEOPLE LIVE AS THOUGH FORGIVENESS WERE A SYSTEM. Two systems of forgiveness exist among divorced people.

System 1: Sentimental forgiveness. "Kiss and make up" is a common element in many relationships; but "kiss and make up" can be premature so that we never address the real issues that led to the wounding. Many people settle for shallow, surface forgiveness rather than giving the time and energy to work to the bedrock of the issues. No wonder the issues reoccur. The goal in this system is to get to the "and-they-all-lived-happily-ever-after" point. But you can't "live happily" with little seedlings of resentment scattered throughout your life.

Forgiveness is like pizza home delivery: no good if it is cold!

 Below describe one incident of sentimental forgiveness in your life.

_____

System 2: Martyrdom forgiveness. The elephant is supposed to have a long memory; well, a lot of divorced people have the elephant beat. We have instant recall and cross-referencing. Just give me a code word and watch the memory spit out the offenses by category. We are cataloguers who find no offense too small to file away for future recall. The goal of this forgiveness is to be able to remind, "I'll forgive you but I won't forget it."

We find no offense too small to file away for future recall.

 Below describe one incident in your life of the martyrdom-system of forgiveness.

_____

Rather than either of these systems, forgiveness has to be authentic. The authentic forgiver says, "But because of what Jesus has done for me, because of how He has forgiven me, I forgive you." The goal of this style of forgiveness is to be like Jesus.

✎ **In the margin describe one incident in your life that reflects the authentic style of forgiveness.**

Forgiveness will be some of the toughest work you do in divorce recovery. You cannot complete the work of divorce recovery if your interior is crowded with anger, resentment, and unforgiveness. By not forgiving your ex, you are hurting yourself. Forgiveness is a decision. I choose to forgive or I choose not to forgive. Each choice has consequence—consequences that also may impact my health, my children, and my future.

Not even _____ will be able to limit or defeat God's plan for me.

Weekly Work

▥➡ **Repeat the affirmation that appears at left.**

Today's objective:
I will accept God's forgiveness as a divorced individual.

Accepting God's Forgiveness

Why are some of us so reluctant to accept God's gift of forgiveness? We find four basic groups among the divorced community.

1. THE ANARCHISTS. Anarchists live by no rules; anything goes in terms of sex, alcohol, or partying. They shuck responsibilities, such as child support or visitation, like a bad-fitting suit. Some anarchists have been hurt and in their anger declare, "Two can play this game."

2. THE PITY-ISTS. Pityists want to tell everyone, everywhere how bad "my" divorce is. Of the one million divorces each year, mine is the worst. No detail is too small to drag under a microscope and magnify. Their theme song is "Poor Me." They want lots of sympathy.

3. THE REVENGERS. Revengers have one goal: helping "the grapes of wrath" ripen. They plot revenge, and when revenge is not easily available, they raid the ex's happiness. "Dirty tricks" such as unsigned alimony checks (which have to be returned) or failing to pick up/return the children on time (which complicates the life of the custodial parent) are part of their well-stocked arsenals.

4. THE COMPETITORS. The competitors do not recognize the finality of the divorce decree, so they work to settle the score or to up the ante. They say, "If the ex gets a new car—I have to have a new car. If the ex buys the child a pony, I'll buy the child a horse." The theme song is, "No one out-loves me."

What do these groups of divorced people have in common? They have not nestled down into the forgiving grace of God. The statement appearing in the margin also describes them.

Some people may have dipped their little toes in the stream of forgiveness but never would consider diving off the high diving board to experience the depth of His grace.

Which group applies to you? Fill in the blanks below.
Early in the divorce I belonged to the _____
Currently, I belong to the _____
What changed you? _____

Forgiveness should be at the top of every divorced person's agenda. Where is it on your agenda? Top? Middle? Or bottom? Have you scheduled forgiveness for "when I get around to it?" or "when (but not until) he/she asks?"

Let's inventory the recipients of forgiveness. To know who needs forgiveness, simply ask who the divorce has touched.

In the exercise below write in the left column the names of all people (you may need extra paper for this exercise) your divorce directly impacts: you, your ex, children, your siblings, in-laws, friends, minister, lawyer, neighbors, the other woman, the other man, etc. Then in the right column write in that person's current attitude toward you: supportive, nonsupportive, neutral, angry, etc.

Person	Attitude
1._____	1._____
2._____	2._____
3._____	3._____
4._____	4._____
5._____	5._____
6._____	6._____
7._____	7._____
8._____	8._____
9._____	9._____
10._____	10._____

See why divorce is not just a small issue? If 1.1 million divorces occur this year, that translates into 2.2 million husbands and wives and X number of children plus four parents. Then you add friends, siblings, neighbors, colleagues at work. Pretty soon it becomes like the rock tossed in the pond—the ripple touches a lot of shoreline. Sometimes, individuals that we are not aware of are touched.

Go through your list and put a star by those who need your forgiveness. Go through the list and put an asterisk by those whom you need to ask for forgiveness.

I'll bet you forgot to list yourself. You may say, *But I'm the innocent party in this thing!* All the more reason you too need forgiveness. Because if you feel forgiven, if forgiveness is a present-tense reality in your life, it is such a blessing, you will want others to know forgiveness.

Here are some suggestions in regard to forgiveness:
1. Ask God to forgive you for what you have done. Then forgive yourself for what you have done. Do you need to pray one of these or other prayers?
- God, forgive me for acting arrogantly and not being willing to go to counseling.
- God, forgive me for not wanting reconciliation.

- God, forgive me for not speaking up for my needs so my spouse could know how I felt.
- God, forgive me for spending too much time being busy instead of spending time learning to have intimate conversations.

Luke 15 tells one of the most famous stories in the Bible—the story of the prodigal son. As Jesus told the story, He reported about the prodigal son: (v. 17), "When he came to his senses . . . ." Some of us, when we have come to our senses, after a divorce—sometimes, long after the divorce—have been stunned by the emotional carnage we have created. Have you really owned up to your responsibility for what you did to create this divorce?

Some of us are stunned by the emotional carnage we have created.

✎ **Have you made a decision or said a few choice things when you were angry that you now regret? Describe one of these moments.**

_____

What have you done to deal with the incident? _____

_____

If you do not own up to responsibility for your actions, you will race into a spouse search. Or you may race into a behavioral choice to "drown out" your pain. God will, I believe, bring opportunities for forgiveness into our lives.

✎ **Answer the questions below.**
Has God forgiven you? ❏ Yes ❏ No ❏ Uncertain
What makes you certain? _____
What makes you uncertain? _____

If you cannot say God has forgiven you, would now be a good time to ask Him for forgiveness? Remember this verse: "If we confess our sins, he is faithful and just and will forgive us our sins and purify us from all unrighteousness" (1 John 1:9).

✎ **Answer the following questions:**
Have you forgiven yourself? ❏ Yes ❏ No ❏ Unsure
Are you willing to forgive yourself? ❏ Yes ❏ No
Have you asked God to help you forgive yourself? ❏ Yes ❏ No
Are you willing to ask God now to help you forgive yourself?
❏ Yes ❏ No

2. Ask God to forgive you for what you have felt. Maybe you've hated your ex. You have systematically worked to turn others against your ex. Maybe you have ignored signs of support and believe that your church did not accept you. Sometimes our feelings do not match reality; we often rearrange reality to support our feelings.

3. Ask God to forgive you for what you have thought. Sometimes we have by our thoughts created some of the sins of our exes; we have misinterpreted their actions, we have questioned their intentions. We have not given them opportunity to explain, or we have not listened to their explanations.

4. Ask God to forgive you for what you have desired. What have you desired, wished for, longed for, fantasized about? Your ex to get cancer? Have

Sadly, some of us have been tougher on ourselves than God has been. We need to admit that we don't play God so well.

a heart attack? Your kids to totally reject your ex? For his "sweetie" to ditch him? We need to bring our desires under the umbrella of forgiveness.

5. Ask God to forgive you for what you have been. Have you been tough? Stubborn? Have you overplayed the "wronged" spouse part? Read the comment appearing in the margin.

This business of forgiveness is difficult work. This process may be most uncomfortable; we are better at pointing out the sins and mistakes and failures of others than we are at recognizing ours. We need help. God offers that in generous portions through the Holy Spirit.

➠ **Stop and pray. Fill in the margin box; then ask forgiveness for areas in your life in which you feel this needs to occur:**

Weekly Work

✎ **Repeat this week's memory verse. Think about three ways God has worked to your good.**

➠ **Go back to page 93 and the names you identified as needing your forgiveness or names of people you need to forgive. Select three names from that list. Now take a moment and pray. Ask God to show you things you could do today to make forgiveness a reality with/for them.**

God, I need forgiveness. Forgive me for—

_____

_____

_____

_____

DAY 5

Today's objective:
I will give serious reflection to the future to which God is calling me.

When Joshua was old and well advanced in years, the Lord said to him, "You are very old, and there are still very large areas of land to be taken over."
–Joshua 13:1

Knowing Where You Are Going

Tony Campolo has made the phrase, "It's Friday, but Sunday's a coming!" well appreciated. The reality behind the phrase is that Easter Sunday (resurrection) follows Good Friday (crucifixion). You've had your crucifixion (divorce)—that's past tense. You may fear that your resurrection (divorce recovery) is permanently delayed.

Where will you be when you get to where you are going? Recovery or more pain? The choices we make determine our eventual destinations. I believe that some of us make some right turns, left turns, and enter a few cul-de-sacs en route. But if we keep on the road to recovery, eventually we will reach the destination. Here are some choices we can make in that process:

CHOICE 1: A BIG WHIFF OF REALITY. One of my favorite verses is Joshua 13:1, which appears in the margin. The *Revised Standard Version* says, ". . . there remains yet very much land to be possessed." The *Living Bible* uses the term *conquered*. You too, although divorced, have lands yet to be possessed or conquered—dreams yet to be achieved. The Lord is not through with you because of this experience. God is not anxious for you to remain in the present. He beckons you to a future. Jeremiah 29:11 contains His promise: "'For I know the plans I have for you,' declares the Lord, 'plans to prosper you and not to harm you, plans to give you hope and a future.'" This is a "double-barreled" promise: a hope AND a future.

What would a "future" have to include for you to consider it "good"? Below write your answer.

_____

_____

You may have written something like this: *To call my future good, it would have to include an attitude of reduced bitterness about my spouse. I would call my future good if I could get back to pursuing my career, which I had to abandon during the divorce.*

CHOICE 2: LOOK TO THE FUTURE RATHER THAN THE PAST. Some of us have strained necks—we walk forward but with our eyes swiveled to the side trying to keep the past in focus. Read the quote appearing at left. The word *everything* includes our divorces. God's grace sustains us in our hardships, and we can put our trust in Him for the future.

Maybe you now regret some choices you made about your divorce. Maybe you wish that you had given reconciliation a better shot. Maybe you realize that your hardness of heart influenced the divorce. God can deal with all your "if only's." The most beautiful windows in the world are made from broken pieces of glass that a master crafter shaped. God specializes in creating futures out of broken pasts. Why should you be an exception?

Read Psalm 34:18 in the margin at left. In the box under the verse describe how this verse speaks to you.

You may have written something like this: "This verse indicates that God is aware of my crushed spirit and will not forget me. It helps me see that I do not have to be whole for God to be close to me or for me to be close to Him."

CHOICE 3: FOCUS ON THE OPPORTUNITY—Divorce becomes an opportunity because God is with us. Fears keep divorced people from seeing and seizing the future which comes in chunks called "opportunities." The Bible tells us through its powerful stories—often set in less-than-desirable locales like wildernesses, deserts, prisons, slavery, bellies of a whale, hog pens, with only an occasional palace—that God is there. Your divorce may resemble a wilderness. The wilderness does not frighten God.

Kathy's husband ran off with Kathy's best friend. He filed for divorce. He and the new woman in his life married two days after the divorce was final. For the next two years Kathy was in and out of hospitals dealing with gastrointestinal difficulties that doctors said were related to stress. Because of repeated absences for illness, Kathy lost her job.

To learn to cope with the difficulties in her life, Kathy joined a support group at her church. Today she has quit smoking, lost almost 100 pounds, and monitors carefully the types of food she eats. She is experiencing her best health in years. A member of her support group knew of a job opening in his office and helped Kathy gain new employment in an affirming environment. Kathy began learning new assertiveness and boundary-setting skills that helped her form stronger relationships. The divorce—an event that she thought would devastate her life forever—ended up as a blessing.

We can view everything that happens in life—the joyous as well as the difficult—as a potential gift to us.

The Lord is close to the broken-hearted and saves those who are crushed in spirit.

–Psalm 34:18

How this verse speaks to me—

_____

_____

_____

_____

The wilderness of your divorce does not frighten God.

I certainly am not saying that divorces are blessings. But I am saying that Scripture teaches that in all things God works.

CHOICE 4: KEEP YOUR ARMS AND HEART OPEN. Life has a wonderful way of delivering surprises and blessings. You say, "Oh, sure. When my ship comes in, with my luck, I'll be at the airport." The figures below illustrate the three ways I can choose to live.

welcoming   skeptical   defensive

_____   _____   _____

 In the space below the description, write in the word "past" to show which figure depicts you at the time of your divorce. Write in "post-divorce" for the figure that best depicts you after your divorce. Now write in "present" in the space that best represents how you are now. You possibly may write two or even three descriptions under the same character.

I can stand with my arms folded across my chest and dare life to approach me. Or I can choose to stand with my arms wide open. If I do the latter, someone could hit me in the stomach, but I prefer to expect that someone will walk into my arms and hug me. We even could depict some divorced people as having their hands clinched in fists because they are so angry. We cannot receive gifts when our hands are clinched.

The bottom is solid

The late Urban Holmes, formerly dean of the University of the South, related the story of a brilliant professor whose son was killed in an accident. The distraught professor disappeared but returned one evening for a seminary banquet and asked if he could say a few words. "Ladies and gentlemen," he began, "in the last few weeks I have been to the bottom." He paused to regain his emotions. "But I am happy to report that the bottom is solid."[5]The testimony of thousands of divorced individuals is that through the grace of God, they too have discovered that the bottom is solid in the tough times.

CHOICE 5: CHOOSE YOUR OWN DIRECTION. All of us get the chance to stand at the forks of the road and choose. You may lose some divorced friends when you choose the high road in your divorce recovery; you may have to ignore a lot of unsolicited advice urging you to get even, to settle some scores with an ex, to "live it up." Ask God to direct your paths.

CHOICE 6: TRUST THE GOD WHO NEVER FAILS. How can you survive this divorce experience? By leaning your whole weight on Jesus. He will accompany us through the ups and downs, the right turns and the left turns (perhaps even some U-turns) of divorce recovery.

CHOICE 7: FOCUS ON THE FATHER, NOT ON THE CRISES. Ken Smith once reminded me that Jesus survived so many crises because He focused on the Father, not on the crises. In His last hours He prayed, "Father, glorify your name!" (John 12:28). Dare we pray the same? Dare we invite God to be glorified in recovery from divorce?

CHOICE 8: DO SOMETHING! The following exercise may most effectively wrap up these six agendas.

✎ **Answer the questions below.**

1. What do I want to do with the life I have left? _____

    _____

2. What do I want to learn? _____

3. What do I want to be part of? _____

4. What do I want to change, shape, leave better than I found it? _____

    _____

Hopefully, you will seize the opportunity to accommodate the priorities God has for you. Some of us can be in the right place but looking for the wrong thing. Now would be a great time to look not for Mr. or Miss Right II. Now would be a great time to look for God's best and God's will.

Finally, God still gives wisdom. Some divorced people feel that God no longer will be active in their lives. God still leads—even more so when we have failed but have faced that failure and confessed it. He redeems the path.

Facing the Future

"Where do I go from here?"

As you complete the six core agendas of *A Time for Healing,* you may find yourself asking, "Where do I go from here?" You may desire to continue your growth through further study. Several options are available to you. We highly encourage your entire group to continue to study the remaining three (optional) agendas in this workbook, but even if your entire group is unable to continue, you and two or three group members could continue to meet to discuss the final three agendas. Strongly consider studying agenda 9, "Some Biblical Dimensions", if you can add only one additional agenda to your schedule. If you are not already involved in a regular Bible study at your church, such as a weekly Sunday School class or a weekly discipleship group, you may find that regular focus on God's Word to be important in your life. You may want to learn to lead support groups in your church so you can share your growth experience with others, or you may want to talk to a church staff member about a way you can use your new understanding of and commitment to Christ to teach a Bible study or to serve the Lord in some other way in your church.

Beyond that, you can benefit from one of the following resources, all of which are written in the interactive format you have used as you studied *A Time for Healing.* All of these books are intended for group study along with daily, individual work. Determine a particular area in which you need to grow. Then use one or more of these resources to help you continue your spiritual growth.

To build your self-worth on the forgiveness and love of Jesus Christ:
- *Search for Significance* LIFE₍ᵣ₎ Support Group Series Edition by Robert S. McGee, Johnny Jones, and Sallie Jones (Houston: Rapha Publishing). This study helps you replace the four false beliefs with principles of truth from God's Word. Member's Book (0805499903); Leader's Guide (080549989X).

To identify and replace codependent behaviors:
- *Untangling Relationships: A Christian Perspective on Codependency* by Pat Springle and Susan A. Lanford (Houston: Rapha Publishing). This course helps individuals understand codependency and learn how to make relationships more healthy. Member's Book (0805499733); Leader's Guide (0805499741).

- *Conquering Codependency: A Christ-Centered 12-Step Process* by Pat Springle and Dale W. McCleskey (Houston: Rapha Publishing). The learned perceptions and behaviors called codependency—the compulsion to rescue, help, and fix others—often add to our addictive behaviors. *Conquering Codependency* applies the Christ-centered 12 Steps to these habits. Member's Book (080549975X); Facilitator's Guide, available for free download at *www.lifeway.com/discipleplus/download.htm*.

To help you grow in developing a healthy lifestyle:
- *Fit 4: A LifeWay Christian Wellness Plan* (Nashville: LifeWay Press). Making one healthy choice after another means being fit in all four areas of life—heart, soul, mind, and strength. This wellness plan blends taking care of your body, being devoted to God, and maintaining healthy relationships with family, friends, and others. *Nutrition Starter Kit* (063300581); *Fitness Starter Kit* (0633005827).

To understand God's will for your life:
- *Experiencing God: Knowing and Doing the Will of God* by Henry Blackaby and Claude V. King (Nashville: LifeWay Press). Find answers to the often-asked question "How can I know and do God's will?" This study helps Christians discover God's will and obediently follow it. Member's Book (0805499547); Leader's Guide (0805499512).

To help you develop your prayer life:
- *Disciple's Prayer Life: Walking in Fellowship with God* by T. W. Hunt and Catherine Walker (Nashville: LifeWay Press). This course helps adults learn to pray through experiences based on prayers of the Bible. Its sessions offer practical experiences that strengthen and deepen prayer lives and help churches develop an intercessory prayer ministry. (0767334949).

To learn more about the Bible:
- *Step by Step Through the Old Testament* by Waylon Bailey and Tom Hudson (Nashville: LifeWay Press). This self-instructional workbook surveys the Old Testament, provides a framework for understanding and interpreting it, and teaches Bible background. Member's Book (0767326199); Leader's Guide (0767326202).

- *Step by Step Through the New Testament* by Thomas D. Lea and Tom Hudson (Nashville: LifeWay Press). This 13-unit self-instructional workbook surveys the New Testament, provides a framework for understanding and interpreting the New Testament, and teaches Bible background. Member's Book (0805499466); Leader's Guide (0767326210).

To help you learn to think the thoughts of Christ:
• *The Mind of Christ* by T. W. Hunt and Claude V. King (Nashville: LifeWay Press). This course is a serious study of what it means to have the thoughts of Christ and to renew the mind, as Scripture commands. Member's Book (0805498702); Leader's Guide (0805498699).

To help you learn how to disciple others:
• *MasterLife* by Avery T. Willis, Jr. (Nashville: LifeWay Press). This discipleship process guides both new and experienced believers to develop lifelong, obedient relationships with Jesus Christ. It is recommended that participants complete all four six-week studies in sequence, but any book can be studied independently. Videos are strongly recommended. Leader Kit (0767326407).

To equip you to witness to others:
• *Witnessing Through Your Relationships* by Jack R. Smith and Jennifer Kennedy Dean (Nashville: LifeWay Press). This 12-unit course teaches you how to evaluate a lost person's receptivity to the gospel, cultivate relationships and build trust, and develop skills for sharing the good news. Member's Book (0805498931); Leader's Guide (0805498923).

To order copies of this resource and the above resources: WRITE LifeWay Church Resources Customer Service, 127 Ninth Avenue, North, Nashville, TN 37234-0113; FAX order to (615) 251-5933; PHONE 1-800-458-2772; EMAIL to *CustomerService@lifeway.com*; ONLINE at *www.lifeway.com*; or visit the LifeWay Christian Store serving you.

We heartily congratulate you for completing the core units of this workbook. Thank you for having the courage and tenacity to look at these issues squarely and to vow to tackle them with God's help.

Weekly Work

▐▶ **Repeat three times this week's memory verse.**

▐▶ **Repeat the affirmation appearing in the margin.**

> *Not even my own failures will be able to defeat God's plan and love for me, especially if I accept His gracious forgiveness.*

Notes
[1]Jason Towner, *Warm Reflections*, (Nashville: Broadman, 1977), 60.
[2]Frank E. Graeff, "Does Jesus Care?" ©1901.
[3]Ibid.
[4]Frank Eifert, "People Cared—But Not Like Jesus," *Herald of Holiness*, 1 April 1989, 12-13.
[5]Urban T. Holmes III, *Spirituality for Ministry*, (San Francisco: Harper & Row, 1982), 135. Used by permission of Mrs. Urban T. Holmes III.

Reviewing Holiday Traditions

This week's agenda:
You will review holiday traditions and celebrations.

FAITHFUL IN A NEW WAY

Regina told this story: "I really couldn't understand how a God of love, harmony, and reconciliation was letting my marriage come crashing down around my ears. I thought it was up to God to keep it together, not to let it fall apart. I was upset with God for a good while, and yet I needed the Holy Spirit so desperately: for comfort, wisdom, consolation, and hope. God was my all and all, and in God's arms I often cried myself to sleep.

"Many people had commented on how God had helped them through the more difficult parts of life. Now it was my turn to realize the reality of God's presence. There were so many things with which I felt that I couldn't cope. Simple things were a horrendous effort when I had to do it all in the midst of unmeasurable depression. But I began to find God faithful in a new way. The money for the rent always came in. The patient load at the office increased without any effort on my part. And we had peace at home."[1]

What can we learn from Regina's testimony that would enable us to turn everything—even holiday traditions—over to God? In this chapter we'll discover that God wants to be Lord over all—even holiday traditions.

What you will learn

This week you will—
• discover how divorce and recovery impact holidays and celebrations;
• reexamine holiday traditions you had before the divorce;
• learn strategies for finding meaning in new traditions;
• create a new day for celebration: A Doxology Day;
• learn the healing capacity of nurturing yourself through celebration.

What you will study

Living with Holidays	Traditions and Celebrations	New Ways to Celebrate	Creating a Doxology Day	Nurturing First-Person Singular
DAY 1	DAY 2	DAY 3	DAY 4	DAY 5

Memory verse

This week's verses of Scripture to memorize—
Bless the Lord, O my soul; and all that is within me, bless His holy name! Bless the Lord, O my soul, and forget none of His benefits.

—Psalms 103:1-2, NASB

Living with Holidays

Today's objective:
I will discover how holidays/celebrations impact divorce and recovery.

Have you gone through your first Christmas yet as a divorced person? Do you remember your first "divorced" Christmas?

 Fill in the blanks below.

In a word, that first Christmas was _____

That was mainly because _____

At holiday time, advertisements and commercials featuring the two-parent home surround us. Christmas cards and other holiday images project families in which both a mom and dad always are present. Such ads feature families piling into cars for their Christmas trips with no stops along the way to drop children off at the home of the noncustodial parent. Such images depict a storybook setting that does not represent families in which a divorce has occurred.

Bah, humbug!
—Ebenezer Scrooge,
single adult

Holidays are like the big "focus" spots used in talent shows; sometimes you see more than you want to see. Holidays are a blend of imperfect people, complicated life circumstances, and expectations that are impossible to attain. The blend sometimes has disastrous results. Like fruitcake, a lot of other ingredients get mixed in:
• people with strong opinions
• people who remember the way "it used to be"
• people with major-league expectations and minor-league budgets
• people with lots of unprocessed baggage
• people with hidden emotional agendas

 In the spaces that follow list the three holidays that currently are the most difficult for you.

#1 most difficult: _____

Why? _____

#2 most difficult: _____

Why? _____

#3 most difficult: _____

Why? _____

Here are some key points to remember about holidays:

Holidays are a time to be on the emotional offensive—to guard your heart and your checkbook.

KEY POINT #1: DON'T IGNORE THE HOLIDAYS OR "RED LETTER" OCCASIONS. Divorced people without children want to "fast-forward" over holidays; those with children can feel like they are taking the Fourth Division on maneuvers—lots of logistics to be worked out, not to mention compromises, concessions, and some emotional bruises. In all probability, somewhere in the divorce agreement are clauses about holidays and other special days. So, your holiday plans are complicated. You couldn't get along with this person while you were married to her/him. Now you have to decide how every holiday is to be celebrated. You realize that if this one is bungled, the next holiday on the horizon becomes more complicated.

Anticipate the holidays and "red-letter" days on your personal calendars. Don't wait until the last minute to decide what to do. Think. Plan. If you have children, involve them. Be creative and imaginative.

KEY POINT #2: "CENSOR" THE ADS, COMMERCIALS AND INVITATIONS TO SPEND YOUR WAY THROUGH THIS HOLIDAY. Turn on the TV and "special" holiday-themed commercials go directly for your emotional jugular and for your wallet.

The reality is that if you don't buy it for your child(ren), your ex might. Especially if he/she knows—and the children will help their other parent know—that you said no. Children from single-parent homes add a whole new dimension to consumer persuasion. Indeed, they may point out, politely or arrogantly, "Dad/Mom will get it for me."

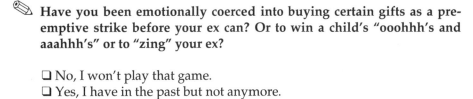 **Have you been emotionally coerced into buying certain gifts as a pre-emptive strike before your ex can? Or to win a child's "ooohhh's and aaahhh's" or to "zing" your ex?**

❑ No, I won't play that game.
❑ Yes, I have in the past but not anymore.
❑ Yes, because _____

Impress them on your children. Talk about them when you sit at home and when you walk along the road, when you lie down and when you get up. Tie them as symbols on your hands and bind them on your foreheads. Write them on the doorframes of your houses and on your gates.

–Deuteronomy 6:7-8

Read Deuteronomy 6:7-8 appearing in the margin. Moses refers to the command to "Love the Lord your God with all your heart and with all your soul and with all your strength" (v. 5), but the principle applies to the ways we deal with family decisions. Because of our faith and because of our financial realities, this particular holiday or special day may have to be radically different than previous ones.

Use these "teachable" moments to reach your children's hearts. Don't make promises you can't deliver. Some commercials create a wonderful teaching opportunity to help children separate the reality from the hype in TV advertisements, especially at holiday time.

KEY POINT #3: WATCH YOUR AGENDA. Holidays and red-letter days on your family calendar can be wonderful opportunities to encourage healing or to "salt" the wounds and "sandpaper" old scars. It's your choice! If some

Escalating the stakes

unfinished business exists between you and your ex, it's like the proverbial "chip on the shoulder" waiting to be bumped. Don't add more chips.

Are you tempted to try to "make it up" to your family or to your children? Credit-card companies love for you to do just that (at 18 per cent or higher interest, of course). Are your gift choices "calculated" to win points—to one-up an ex's gifts? Will your giving this time only escalate the stakes next time?

KEY POINT #4: ASK YOURSELF: TO PROMOTE RECOVERY, WHAT DO I REALLY NEED THIS HOLIDAY OR OCCASION TO BE? Thinking through this question and being sure of your answer could lead to you putting love and joy back into your season through some new celebrations or traditions, and you might actually enjoy the occasion. Have you ever wondered what it would be like as a divorced person to enjoy Christmas or Valentine's Day?

Some celebrations and holidays are tough and bittersweet. You'll need extra supplies of tissue. But, in our secular culture, we have so commercialized our holidays and celebrations that we have stripped many of them of their meaning. This might be the time to begin to redeem the holiday or celebration and to bring it in line with your needs.

 Go back to the drawing on page 102. Circle the billboard with the message you will use as your direction during the next holiday you encounter.

Sometimes, through tears, we must say a sad goodbye to traditions just as we have to those with whom we have shared those traditions! But each goodbye is an opportunity to say hello to a new way to celebrate.

Weekly Work

 Write in the margin three times this week's memory verse.

 Repeat the affirmation appearing at left.

Traditions and Celebrations

Some of us have selective memories. Some divorced people "remember" previous holiday celebrations and traditions as wonderful; since the divorce everything is the pits. Give 'em a couple of bars of "I'll Be Home for Christmas" or Elvis' "I'll Have A Blue Christmas Without You," and they are emotional basket cases. Here are some more steps we can take regarding traditions and celebrations:

ACTION STEP #1. TAKE A FRESH LOOK AT YOUR TRADITIONS AND WAYS OF CELEBRATING. Are yourself, Do I really enjoy all the holiday rituals that I feel I must maintain year after year? How much do these ways of celebrating actually mean to me? Do they fit with my life circumstances now, or are they past relics that need to be rethought?

✎ **Below describe one tradition or custom or a celebration that you observed when you were married.**

_____

DAY 2

Today's objective:
I will reexamine holiday traditions as they were before the divorce.

How did it get started? _____

Do you really miss it or "kinda" miss it? _____
Now think of one tradition that you have not missed. Why have you not

missed it? _____

Some males while married just took all the preparations for granted. Now single, they appreciate it more but are celebration-impaired.

Actually, women carry out (or execute) many of the traditions. Some males while married just took all the preparations for granted. Now single, they appreciate it more but are celebration-impaired. What wonderful opportunity for them to learn celebration logistics! Some single moms find they do not miss all the hours and energy spent in pulling off a "Norman Rockwell" type holiday. Now, they can enjoy the holiday, too.

ACTION STEP #2: CRITIQUE THE TRADITIONS. Ask yourself and your children some questions:
• Did we really enjoy past celebrations?
• How do our friends celebrate? Your children have friends in one-parent or blended families and will have some suggestions of how other families celebrate special days and events.

Change naturally creates emotional discomfort during emotion-laden holidays.

If you initiate a new tradition, critique it. Some will need a little fine-tuning or adjusting or getting used to. In critiquing the traditions, listen to everyone and consider their points of view. That may mean some ground rules: No "I wish we were doing it the old way!" Or set a time limit on sulking. Such behaviors, if not directed, can sabotage the new celebration getting a fair start. You even hear, "I am going to be miserable, no matter what!" Holidays are so emotion-laden. Change—particularly forced change—naturally creates emotional discomfort, as do economic realities.

✎ **Think of one idea you always have wanted to try for a holiday or personal celebration. Perhaps your spouse was resistant. In the space below describe it.**

I have always wanted to try _____

What keeps me from trying it now? _____

_____

What would be necessary for me to do to start it this year? _____

_____

ACTION PLAN #3. PLAN AHEAD. Don't wait until the day before an event/holiday to begin asking for suggestions. You will need to discuss with your ex some ideas about children's gifts for his or her input (but not necessarily his or her veto). Everyone will need time to mull over some ideas, although you may not have 100-percent enthusiasm or cooperation.

ACTION PLAN #4. BE REASONABLE. Holidays and celebrations, like birthdays/graduations, easily can become the arena for friendly—or unfriendly—competition for exes, particularly when unfinished business exists between them. Some single parents desire to "make it up" to the children for "all they've been through." Some children sense this and manipulate you. They will ask for outlandish gifts and will pit you against your ex. I've seen single parents go all out for Christmas and then be broke until Easter.

A divorce can devastate charge accounts. If you gave generously to your children and friends in previous years, how can you face Christmas or birthday giving on a diminished scale? Recognize the subtle temptation to overspend in order to bolster your wounded ego.

ACTION PLAN #5: ANTICIPATE THE BITTERSWEET. Family occasions can be particularly difficult when ex-spouses share custody. Children scheduled to be with the other parent on the particular day (or days) may make that day "blue" for you. It's OK to feel blue, but you need to reach out to friends. Don't play the "if-only" symphony or rehash—in slow motion—memories of previous celebrations. Some families do not sign "cease-fire" agreements for holidays. The holidays merely provide new insults to be exchanged. Take a moment and realize that your ex may be hurting, too.

Bring the bittersweet to God and ask for His help. Some divorced people have found elements missed in previous holiday celebrations as a married person. Sadly, for too many, coping with celebration itself overshadows the reason for the observance.

➡ **Stop and pray the prayer below. As you pray, fill in the blank with the name of the holiday or observance that most troubles you.**

O God, you know I have difficulty with _____ (specific holiday/occasion). I know it is a time for celebration, but it is especially difficult for me. Give me some fresh ideas and the courage to celebrate this day. Amen.

Weekly Work

✎ **In the margin write what this week's memory verses mean to you in light of your present circumstances in divorce recovery.**

➡ **Repeat the affirmation appearing at left.**

New Ways to Celebrate

Some of us are in a celebration rut. Your divorce could be an invitation to create and enjoy new celebrations or even styles of celebrating.

ACTION STEP #1: START SOME NEW TRADITIONS. This could be the year for a totally new tradition because so many "memory triggers" tie us to the past rather than to the future. Christmas ornaments or the absence of particular Christmas ornaments, for example, might be all it takes to drop you several notches emotionally.

For example, traditionally have you spent the two days before Christmas baking "the feast" for/with a houseful of relatives? Did you really enjoy that?

Sometimes, through tears, we must say a sad goodbye to traditions just as we have to those with whom we have shared those traditions! But each goodbye is an opportunity to say hello to a new way to celebrate.

DAY 3

Today's objective:
I will learn strategies for finding meaning in new traditions.

Becky did that for years—with little more than a "Good meal, hon" from her husband, who spent most of the day glued to the football games on TV. Since the divorce she and the girls have pizza on holidays. "As a single mom, I don't spend my time in the kitchen 'slaving' over a meal the girls will pick at. So we order a big pizza and have a great time together. Maybe we will do turkey when they are older," she says.

Sing to the Lord a new song; sing to the Lord, all the earth.

–Psalm 96:1

If you are a single parent, you will have to consider logistics. Is it your year to have the children Christmas Day? What if you traditionally have opened presents Christmas Eve? Make Christmas Day the event! Maybe it is the year to eat out rather than confront memories of the traditional gatherings around the table. How about a Christmas picnic?

 Read the week's affirmation that appears below. Underline the key words that challenge you:

Sometimes, through tears, we must say a sad goodbye to traditions just as we have to those with whom we have shared those traditions! But each goodbye is an opportunity to say hello to a new way to celebrate.

What do these words mean to you? _____

_____

You may have written something like this: "It's OK to be sad about saying goodbye to traditions and the people with whom we observed them, but we can replace them with things that may be just as meaningful, if not more so." Some of us are not overly creative, so we may need help. Go to the library and look up holiday books; even if it is July, now is a good time to calmly plan. Ask single friends how they celebrate holidays and special occasions.

Get help from library books about holidays.

ACTION STEP #2: ASK FOR HELP. When I was married, selecting and decorating the Christmas tree was a joint project. That first year, decorating a tree solo drained me. I was tempted to take a "time out" until January 1, but I was on the admissions staff of a college in North Carolina. As we planned a holiday reception, I volunteered my home. So I had to decorate. That proved to be a good decision and helped me get through that Christmas alone.

Ask friends to help you decorate. One year, when I decided not to decorate, one friend showed up with a live tree and demanded, "Where do you keep your decorations?" He decorated the tree for me as his gift. It now grows in my backyard as I write.

Decorating was just another reminder of my loss.

Solo decorating can be bittersweet. I've at times lost my temper trying to get the tree straight in the tree stand as I thought about past years and how helpful Jane's hands were in steadying the tree while I tightened the bolts. I missed Jane helping me. Decorating was just another reminder of my loss. So I had a few minutes to feel the bittersweet before I finished the decorating.

ACTION STEP #3: STAY HOME. Maybe as a married person you always were part of the annual trek to someone's house for Christmas. You spent a great deal of time in a packed car driving and sleeping on someone's couch. You considered but discarded the idea of staying home for Christmas. "Maybe next year." Well, maybe this is "next year."

My first Christmas "solo," I found my parents and family on "eggshells." "Whatever you do, don't mention her name," seemed to be the underlying rule. That only made conversation and memories difficult. Most of the time I felt guilty for dampening everyone's Christmas enthusiasm with my sadness.

Then came the year I decided to stay in Kansas City and celebrate Christmas in my own home, which was difficult for my family to accept. I admit I had a few "second guesses" early on Christmas Eve, but then a friend gave me the gift of a phone call. What a celebration we had catching up!

Yes, eating alone was tough. I had called a restaurant to make a brunch reservation but was told, "We don't do parties of one on Christmas!" I eventually found a restaurant that would take my reservation. En route I had the horrible fear of hearing "Smith . . . PARTY OF ONE!!!" reverberate through the waiting area. *So sad—party of one on Christmas!* But the receptionist merely called, "Smith party" and caught my eye. I kinda gave myself a pat on the back for my courage. I had a fabulous brunch and a wonderful, relaxed Christmas at home.

A pat on the back for courage

 Below identify and write about a time when you deserved a pat on the back for attempting something at a holiday as a single adult.

_____

_____

ACTION STEP #4: GET INVOLVED IN MAKING CHRISTMAS FOR SOMEONE ELSE. One of the great projects in our church at Christmas is the "Joshua" tree. Names of children with special needs hang on a tall tree. The card tells the child's name, age, size, and needs. I picked two cards and headed to the mall to shop for children I will never meet. I bought toys and coats, wrapped them, and placed them under the Joshua tree.

When I lived in California, I had Christmas cookie parties. I baked dozens of sugar cookies, made the icing, and invited friends to a "drop-in" Christmas party. One stipulation: everyone had to decorate some cookies. If you messed up, you ate the cookie and started over. I put people at tables of four and encouraged them to talk about their Christmas memories and traditions. We had a marvelous evening, and the Salvation Army got dozens of creatively decorated cookies for their programs.

I'm lonely, Lord
not missing him,
just all alone
and wanting in
on joy and laughter
two can share . . ..
So Lord, I pray
could you please send a
special Christmas season
friend to ease the
burden and help
celebrate Your day?[6]

Call a social service agency and volunteer for holiday assignment. For example, the kitchens for the homeless always seek volunteers, especially on the holidays. I've even worked in a funeral home on Christmas so that married staff members could have the day off.

ACTION STEP #5: PARTNER AN EVENT. Do you think you will be the only person in your zip code to be alone on this holiday or special occasion? Start asking and broker-up an "everybody-bring-something" potluck dinner. Listen closely for the person who doesn't have Christmas plans. Invite.

ACTION STEP #6: DON'T SEND CHRISTMAS CARDS IF THAT CREATES ANXIETY. WAIT AND SEND VALENTINE DAY CARDS OR A NEWSLETTER INSTEAD.

DAY
4

Today's objective:
I will create a new day for celebration: a Doxology Day.

This is the day the Lord has made; let us rejoice and be glad in it.

–Psalm 118:24

ACTION STEP #7: STOP FOCUSING SO MUCH ON "WHAT THE HOLIDAYS USED TO BE" AND FOCUS ON WHAT THE HOLIDAYS CAN BE! That's sound advice from my friend, Asa Sparks, a counselor in Alabama. In the margin box write three words to describe what your holidays once were and three words to describe what the holidays can be. Here's an important reminder from Niki Scott: "If you feel as if you're the only one in the world whose Christmas won't fit the Hallmark card/TV image of how Christmas should be this year, you're not alone. Most of us feel that way. . . . It also might help to remember that this holiday isn't about where we celebrate—or how. It's about the birth of a Savior who also didn't spend Christmas in a Norman Rockwell setting."[2]

Weekly Work

 Repeat from memory this week's memory verses. Below describe some of His benefits to you.

_____

Creating a Doxology Day

We haven't discussed yet one of the most anxiety-riddled observances of all: the anniversary day. You may ask, "What am I supposed to do about it?" Well, some of us didn't have such a hot record for remembering anniversaries while we were married. Others of us cannot forget the day we married.

 Fill in the blanks below.

My anniversary is/was on _____

How did you celebrate your anniversary the first year you were married?

_____

How did you celebrate your anniversary the last year you were married?

_____

How did you non-celebrate this year?
____ I didn't even think about it.
____ I thought about it for about two seconds.
____ I tried not to think about it.
____ I _____

ACTION PLAN #1: MAKE THE DAY A POSITIVE MEMORY. Read Psalm 118:24 appearing in the margin. As you read it, you might ask, "Rejoice? What do I have to be glad about? This is divorce recovery, remember?" Some possibilities might be your children/grandchildren, your friends, good health, salvation, and a roof over your head.

 For what three things in your life can you thank God right now? On the next page write your answer.

One good thing—

_____

_____

_____

One funny thing—

_____

_____

_____

1. _____
2. _____
3. _____

I suggest that divorced people not try to ignore the anniversary day. Rather, I suggest you remember one good thing and one funny thing that happened while you were married. In the margin box write your answers.

We often cling to the bad memories that crowd out the good. If you concentrate on remembering the good and the funny—however limited—you will be emotionally ahead.

ACTION PLAN #2: PLAN A DOXOLOGY DAY. Elva McAllaster and I have been colleagues for years; we have shared a rich exchange of letters, cards, and musings. She wrote: "Every day of the Christian's life is a doxology day. 'All blessings' happen continually. But what would you think of inventing a new national holiday, a Doxology Day for singles?"[3]

semi-annual birthday— your birthday plus 6 months; for example, if your birthday is on March 16, then celebrate September 16 as your Doxology Day.

Elva suggests that your **semi-annual birthday** be your individual Doxology Day—a day in which you thank God for all His "benefits" and in which you specifically, creatively, and enthusiastically follow the psalmist's instructions to, "Bless the Lord, O my soul; and all that is within me, bless His holy name."

If you were married, you would have an anniversary; perhaps flowers, a meal out, a card, and gift. Why not a Doxology Day? You don't have to wait for greeting-card companies to announce it or for calendar manufacturers to add it to their calendars or products. You can be as creative as you wish. You can involve other people in the celebration or make it a quiet celebration.

You might say, "I don't wanna celebrate! I don't like being divorced, and I don't like having attention paid to my singleness at any time. I'm not about to throw a hypocritical party to celebrate what I hate, to praise God for it!"[4] No one's making you. It's just a suggestion. But remember, God has given us the ability to praise Him in all things. See Philippians 4:11 at left for Paul's opinion. _Whatever_ covers a lot of ground, even divorce.

I have learned to be content whatever the circumstances.

–Philippians 4:11

 Test time. Fill in the blanks below.

The last time I had a good pity party was—
(occasion) _____

The last time I had a good praise party was—
(occasion) _____

What if a rule existed that you couldn't have a pity party without having a praise party to balance it?

ACTION PLAN #3: CELEBRATE! Here are some possible suggestions—a zillion potentials exist—for celebrating Doxology Day.
1. Change your image for the day. Wear a new hair style; don't comb your hair. If you normally wear dark colors, wear bright.
2. Take the day off. Sleep in. Be lazy.
3. Dust off an activity that you have enjoyed but which doesn't quite fit with your current image. Go swing in the park, blow bubbles, or go to the zoo.
4. Send yourself a card, a cake, flowers, or a singing telegram. Act surprised.
5. Do something so outrageous it will leave all your friends befuddled. Most of us cannot remember the last time when we left people scratching their heads and asking, "What's come over him/her?"

In case you've forgotten, you're a child of God.

Look over these suggestions:
- take a mud bath
- go bungee jumping
- hang glide
- rent a motorcycle
- go white-water rafting
- parasail
- parachute out of a plane
- rent a hot-air balloon
- go mountain climbing

What's tempting? Complete the sentence in the margin box. Your assignment is to check out the Yellow Pages to find someone who could help you do this in the next 30 days.

6. Throw a Doxology Day party. Invite close friends to share the day or a meal or an outing with you.

ACTION PLAN #4: COUNT YOUR BLESSINGS. A wonderful old song by Johnson Oatman has that suggestion in its title. Read it below. Maybe it's time for you to audit your "blessing" account.

> *When upon life's billows you are tempest-tossed,*
> *When you are discouraged, thinking all is lost.*
> *Count your many blessings, name them one by one,*
> *And it will surprise you what the Lord has done.*
> *Count your blessings; name them one by one.*
> *Count your blessings; see what God has done.*
> *Count your blessings; name them one by one.*
> *Count your many blessings; see what God hath done.[5]*

✎ **Fill in the blanks below.**

God has blessed me with _____
God is blessing me with _____
God has blessed me with _____
God is blessing me with _____
God has blessed me with _____

Next time you can't go to sleep, count blessings instead. You just may be surprised to discover "what the Lord has done" and is doing. It can lead you to trust Him for the future.

Weekly Work

▥➡ **Repeat the affirmation appearing at left.**

I know it sounds crazy, but I have always wanted to—

_____

_____

_____

_____

Sometimes, through tears, we must say a sad goodbye to traditions just as we have to those with whom we have shared those traditions! But each goodbye is an opportunity to say hello to a new way to celebrate God's goodness, faithfulness, and mercy.

DAY 5

Today's objective:
I will learn the healing capacity of nurturing myself.

Nurturing First-Person Singular

In an age of instant foods and coffee and televisions that don't have to warm up, of deadlines and expiration dates, we are anxious to save time. We talk about a three-year bachelor's degree, early high-school graduation, instant credit through credit cards. We can't even wait for the votes to be counted but accept results with two percent of precincts reporting.

We suffer from the "poverty of impatience." We want it now. Almost three thousand years ago the prophet Isaiah wrote the words appearing on the next page in the margin–words divorced people desperately need to hear and apply. Do you see an asterisk qualifying or limiting the word *those*? Dare we

Those who hope in the Lord will renew their strength. They will soar on wings like eagles; they will run and not grow weary, they will walk and not be faint.

–Isaiah 40:31

I have found God to be faithful—

_____

_____

_____

_____

_____

_____

---

insert the phrase, "The divorced" for *those*? Read it with that phrase: *The divorced who hope in the Lord will renew their strength.* As a divorced person, do you "hope in the Lord"?

Regina told this story of hope: " I really couldn't understand how a God of love, harmony, and reconciliation was letting my marriage come crashing down around my ears. I thought it was up to God to keep it together, not to let it fall apart. I was upset with God for a good while, and yet I needed the Holy Spirit so desperately: for comfort, wisdom, consolation, and hope. God was my all and all, and in God's arms I often cried myself to sleep.

"Many people had commented on how God had helped them through the more difficult parts of life. Now it was my turn to realize the reality of God's presence. There were so many things with which I felt that I couldn't cope. Simple things were a horrendous effort when I had to do it all in the midst of unmeasurable depression. But I began to find God faithful in a new way. The money for the rent always came in. The patient load at the office increased without any effort on my part. And we had peace at home."[6]

Did you catch those wonderful phrases, "Now it was my turn to realize the reality of God's presence" and "I began to find God faithful in a new way"? in the margin box describe what "new ways" you have found God to be faithful.

Regina's words intrigue me: "to realize the reality of God's presence." How many times have we cried out to God and been angered/annoyed/dismayed by the silence? We expect God to be as quick as counter clerks at fast-food chains. Actually, we may be too fatigued emotionally and spiritually to hear God's voice. Our lives revolve around endless lists that say do-do-do.

But are you deliberately scheduling time for yourself? Single parents and divorced people need time to recharge their batteries. "If I don't do, who will?" demanded one divorced woman with three children. "My ex won't!"

Because of our ambivalence toward God during the divorce process, some of us think we have to do it all ourselves. So we run until we drop. The Old Testament prophet Elijah illustrates this point; when Queen Jezebel threatened his life, he ran far away. Look up 1 Kings 19:1-7; we find Elijah so weary that he prayed to die. An angel told him, "Get up and eat," and added, "for the journey is too much for you."

Guess what? This journey to recovery is too much for you, too. You need what Maya Angelou calls "a day away." A time when you "begin to unwrap the bonds which hold (you) in harness."[7] You notify your friends and housemates that you will not be reachable for 24 hours. Single parents may need to modify this.

Here is how Angelou describes her day away: "On the morning I wake naturally, for I will have set no clock, nor informed my body timepiece when it should alarm. I dress in comfortable and casual clothes and leave my house going no place. If I am living in a city, I wander streets, window-shop, or gaze at buildings. I enter and leave public parks, libraries, the lobbies of skyscrapers, and movie houses. I stay in no place for very long.

"On the getaway day I try for amnesia. I do not want to know my name, where I live, or how many dire responsibilities rest on my shoulders. I detest encountering even the closest friend, for then I am reminded of who I am, and

A day away

the circumstances of my life, which I want to forget for a while. Every person needs to take one day away. A day in which one consciously separates the past from the future."[8]

 I already can hear the protests, but let's write them down.

The reason I cannot take a day away is _____
Another reason I cannot take a day away is _____
Now, think a moment before you answer this one:
The real reason I cannot take a day away is _____

Will your children or those to/for whom you feel responsible be any better off if you drop in your tracks? The psalmist urges, "Be (still) and know that I am God" (Psalm 46:10). The human spirit needs to soak in silence. Admittedly, the single parent with sole custody of the children may have to do this on a school day. Perhaps that person only may be able to take a half-day away or two hours away. But it is a way to start.

You protest: *This sounds like something that costs money.* Well, it costs less than seeing a counselor, for sure. Parks on sunny days, picnics on windy days cost little. Many activities in your community are free. You need time alone to nurture your soul. You can say to another single parent, "I will keep your kids for four hours while you get 'away' if you will keep my kids for four hours while I do.' " Invite God to be with you during whatever time you can devote to "away." And you need to thank God afterward for the hours/day "away."

David Heller wrote his doctoral dissertation on what children believe about God. He asked children, "How does God communicate?" Carl, a seven-year-old, answered, "God comes in the silence and He gives different feelings they need . . . Like I'm not afraid of mice anymore because God gave me a non-afraid feeling."[9] The God Who gave Carl a "non-afraid" feeling will bring you gifts, too. But will you be home if He knocks?

Weekly Work

➠ **Repeat the affirmation appearing at left.**

> On your day away you listen, look, touch, taste, and feel. These are actions that do not cost money—luxuries for the emotions and spirit. Look for joy.

> Sometimes, through tears, we must say a sad goodbye to traditions just as we have to those with whom we have shared those traditions! But each goodbye is an opportunity to say hello to a new way to celebrate God's goodness, faithfulness, and mercy.

Notes
[1]Esly Regina Carvalho, "Single Again: On Emotional Recovery," in Mary O'Brien & Claire Christine, eds., *Single Women: Affirming Our Spiritual Journeys,* (Westport, CT: Bergin & Garvey, 1993), 179.
[2]Taken from a column by Niki Scott. Copyright by Universal Press Syndicate.
[3]Elva McAllaster, *Free to be Single,* (Chappaqua, New York: Christian Herald Books, 1979), 275.
[4]Ibid., 278.
[5]Johnson Oatman, Jr., "Count Your Blessings."
[6]Esly Regina Carvalho, "Single Again: On Emotional Recovery," in Mary O'Brien & Claire Christine, eds., *Single Women: Affirming Our Spiritual Journeys,* (Westport, CT: Bergin & Garvey, 1993), 179.
[7]Maya Angelou, *Wouldn't Take Nothing for My Journey Now,* (New York: Random House, 1993), 137.
[8]Ibid., 138.
[9]David Heller, *Just Build the Ark and the Animals Will Come,* (New York: Random House, 1994), 140.

Understanding Sexuality

This week's agenda:
You will reformulate your understanding of sexuality.

CALLED TO A HIGH STANDARD

Linda told this story: "I had a lot of anger toward men after my husband left me, so I slept around a lot—something I really regret. Then I met Mike—a great guy. After about four dates, when he still hadn't made a move (toward sex), I just came right out and asked him, 'Are you gay or something?'

"'No!' he said. I think he was shocked. Then he said, 'I can't sleep around because I am a Christian.' 'Well, so am I', I said. 'I joined the church when I was seven.'

"'Oh, no, it's more than that,' Mike replied. 'It's believing and living the way Christ wants me to live. It's not that I wouldn't want to have sex, but God calls me to a high standard.'"

What do you think happened to Linda as a result of this conversation with Mike? On page 122 you will read more of the story about how she responded to Mike's high standard.

What you will learn

This week you will—
- confront the sexual loss in your life;
- learn how to establish safe and authentic boundaries;
- discover God's wishes for our sexual expression;
- recognize the "hot spots" of temptation;
- know your "no" strategies.

What you will study

Confronting the Sexual Loss	Establishing Boundaries	Discovering God's Wishes	Recognizing Temptation	Knowing "My" No Strategies
DAY 1	DAY 2	DAY 3	DAY 4	DAY 5

Memory verse

This week's verse of Scripture to memorize—
Do you not know that your body is a temple of the Holy Spirit, who is in you, whom you have received from God? You are not your own; you were bought at a price. Therefore honor God with your body.

—1 Corinthians 6:19

DAY 1

Today's objective:
I will confront the sexual loss in my life.

Confronting the Sexual Loss

You may have been divorced a while now. What is going on sexually or not going on sexually? How are you adjusting to your new reality or sexual loss?

Four weeks ago you participated in an attitude assessment; today we'll do a re-test. Without looking back to your earlier test, complete the following. You can compare scores later.

✎ **Take a moment to read through this list. Place a check in the appropriate column for each attitude.**

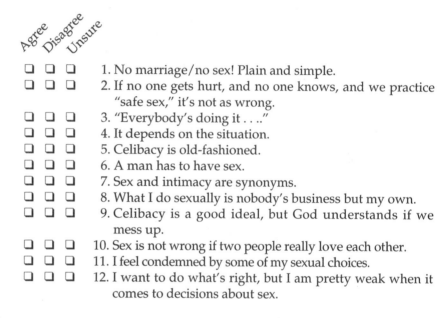

Agree	Disagree	Unsure	
❑	❑	❑	1. No marriage/no sex! Plain and simple.
❑	❑	❑	2. If no one gets hurt, and no one knows, and we practice "safe sex," it's not as wrong.
❑	❑	❑	3. "Everybody's doing it . . .."
❑	❑	❑	4. It depends on the situation.
❑	❑	❑	5. Celibacy is old-fashioned.
❑	❑	❑	6. A man has to have sex.
❑	❑	❑	7. Sex and intimacy are synonyms.
❑	❑	❑	8. What I do sexually is nobody's business but my own.
❑	❑	❑	9. Celibacy is a good ideal, but God understands if we mess up.
❑	❑	❑	10. Sex is not wrong if two people really love each other.
❑	❑	❑	11. I feel condemned by some of my sexual choices.
❑	❑	❑	12. I want to do what's right, but I am pretty weak when it comes to decisions about sex.

Where do we begin to discuss sexuality and divorce? Let's start by reading Genesis 2:25 through 3:13. This encounter between God and the couple called Adam and Eve was not, primarily, about their sexuality. The situation does, however, provide some lessons we can apply to decisions about sex. Here are some key verses in the passage:

God, humankind, and temptation

1. Genesis 2:25: "The man and his wife were both naked, and they felt no shame."
2. Genesis 3:1: "Did God really say, 'You must not eat from the tree in the Garden'?"
3. Genesis 3:7: After Adam and Eve ate, "Then the eyes of both of them were opened, and they realized they were naked."
4. Genesis 3:9: God asked Adam, "Where are you?"
5. Genesis 3:11: God asked Adam, "Who told you that you were naked?"
6. Genesis 3:13: God asked Eve, "What is this you have done?"

Based on these verses about this early relationship of God, humankind, and temptation, here are some questions that we can study in connection with the issues regarding our sexual behavior post-divorce:

QUESTION ONE: DID GOD REALLY *SAY* . . .? The intimacy between Adam and Eve disintegrated with the forbidden fruit of temptation. But first it began with a question. The serpent questioned Eve, "Did God really say, 'You must

We may have been toying with
temptation rather than asking God
for help.

not eat from any tree in the garden?"—an inaccurate paraphrase. What God had told Adam was "You are free to eat from any tree in the garden; but you must not eat from the tree of the knowledge of good and evil . . . (2:16-17)" Do you see the difference? Your "forbidden fruit of temptation" well may occur in the form of an inaccurate question, as well.

The enemy today might paraphrase the question, "Did God really say 'no sex outside of marriage?'" The challenge might come from fellow divorced individuals, many of whom discount a "no" mentality. The quotes in the margin represent a sampling of the wide variety of opinions single individuals have about sexual activity.

The questions or comments may come from our friends or from someone we have dated—someone who pushed for a level of intimacy that made us uncomfortable. Some of their words taunt us:
• You need to get your head out of the sand!
• Everybody does it!
• It's not normal to live without sex!
• Celibate? You've got to be kidding!
• The Bible was written a long time ago!

✎ **Fill in the blanks with some other statements that people have made to you about why you as a divorced person should have sex:**

_____

_____

_____

One man challenged a woman's "no" by citing what he called "the pork law." In essence, he explained to her that the Jews could not eat pork. Why? Because God had forbidden it. Why had God forbidden it? The woman didn't know— but the man with a backlog of hormones explained, "Because they didn't have refrigeration. The pork would spoil and make them sick. But now that we have refrigeration, Jews can eat pork." From there it was only a slight leap to his conclusion that God forbade sex outside of marriage because no birth control existed. But now that we have birth control, we can have sex, he claimed. Well, in that moment, it kinda made sense. Kinda only because two people really wanted to have sex. God said no to sex outside marriage because as the Creator of sex He knew how using sex outside His purposes could wound, hurt, and destroy. The enemy and those who would do his purposes commonly misquote or misinterpret Scripture.

"Then their eyes were opened." Coming to terms with sexuality and intimacy needs, post-divorce, can be a real eye-opener. As one woman said, after her marriage of 26 years ended, "Boy, have things changed since I dated in high school!"

Moreover, like buyer-remorse, you can have "yes remorse" in which you almost want to slap your forehead when you realize, "I could have said no!" Many of us have regrets about sexual choices, especially if we were relying on our own strength. Or, like Eve, we may have been toying with our "forbidden fruit" of temptation rather than asking God for help.

Early in my divorce I wrote the following: The tragedy of failure is to be able to see how close we were to success; that had we repeated our hope one more time, the temptation might have passed and in passing made us stronger for the future. I came so close to success and yet lost. And, in losing, I found my weakness and confessed it.

QUESTION TWO: "WHERE ARE YOU?" (GOD ASKING) Sin makes it difficult to be in a close relationship with God. In the Garden, God often visited the couple "in the cool of the day" (3:8). Yet, that day Adam and Eve were hiding from Him because of their sin. God called out to them, "Where are you?"

God asks us the same question. Where are you on your pilgrimage to recovery? Are your sexual choices keeping you from recovery? from healing? from intimacy with God?

God is not a prude. First, He already knows where we are. Just as He could "see" Adam and Eve in their foliage, he can see us in ours. He confronts us as a way of seeking reconciliation and restoring fellowship with us. God knows. God understands the struggles. Because He loves us, He holds us to a high standard.

God understands

QUESTION THREE: "WHO TOLD YOU THAT YOU WERE NAKED?" Sheepishly, the couple explained that they were in the foliage because they were naked. That prompted God's question. Have you hidden from God in matters pertaining to sex because someone told you you were "old-fashioned" or "prudish" or "out of touch"?

 In the space below, you will find two columns. In the first column list words/phrases others have used to challenge your sexual choices. In the second column, list some of the words/phrases you have used on yourself.

	OTHERS HAVE SAID TO ME	I HAVE SAID TO MYSELF
1.		
2.		
3.		
4.		
5.		

You may have written that people have told you that you will cope with the stress of your divorce better if you yield to your sexual desires. You may have said to yourself something like this: "I deserve to have a fling or two after putting up with my husband's affairs during seven years of marriage."

You need people to support your "no's" rather than shame you for your standards. We sometimes believe that we are the only celibate people in our entire zip code. Oh, others certainly exist, but sometimes people are reluctant to verbalize the same commitment that we have to the high road. Our silence indirectly wounds others.

Sometimes people are reluctant to verbalize the same commitment that we have to the high road.

QUESTION FOUR: "WHAT IS THIS YOU HAVE DONE?" That question asked of our first parents, God asks divorced persons. What is this you have done sexually? God wants to have intimacy with us, even with us as divorced, wounded persons. But we have to be honest if we are to be intimate. When the prophet Nathan challenged King David after his sexual sin with Bathsheba, David owned up and said, "I have sinned against the Lord" (2 Samuel 12:13). We must have such honesty after bad sexual choices, compromises, or "yeses" we now wish we had rejected.

QUESTION FIVE: "DO YOU NOT KNOW THAT YOUR BODY IS A TEMPLE OF THE HOLY SPIRIT?" Our memory verse is the foundation of the apostle Paul's teaching on sexuality. For two reasons, we are not free to do anything we please sexually:
- Our bodies are the temple of the Holy Spirit, who is in us, as a gift from God.
- We are not our own. Although that thought runs contrary to popular culture—we were bought at a price. A high price.

Saying yes to God's best

Paul urges us to "honor" God with our bodies. "This body?" you reply. This body my ex told me was "disgusting!"? This body that he said no one would ever love? This body that I hate? Yes, until there are body transplants, it is the only body you will have. In reality God is not so much asking us to say "NO!" to sex as He is asking us to say "YES!" to the best He has for us.

✎ **Maybe you feel that you are in the "foliage" like Adam, like Eve. Perhaps you are hiding. If so, surely you miss intimacy with God. Maybe something in this material has leaped out at you and you need to spend some time with God. What do you need to tell Him? Fill in the blanks below, and then pray the following prayer:**

God, You know about _____

God, I want You to forgive _____

God, I want You to help me with _____

Weekly Work

✎ **In the margin write this week's memory verse, 1 Corinthians 6:19.**

➠ **Repeat aloud the affirmation appearing at left.**

I want to say "Yes!" to God's best.

DAY 2

Today's objective:
As a divorced adult I will learn how to establish safe and authentic boundaries for sexual expression.

Establishing Boundaries

Boundaries are one of the basic elements of games. We have courts, rinks, rings, fields—generally with fairly precise pregame-determined dimensions and boundaries. That's why you can't play football on a baseball field or soccer on a volleyball court.

Boundaries also apply to sexual intercourse. God has defined the boundaries and is unlikely to change His mind anytime soon. That's His privilege since He invented sex. God has set up boundaries to enhance humankind's enjoyment of this gift, not to frustrate us.

Some people believe that since society is increasingly tolerant of premarital sex and since so many divorced individuals are thoroughly tolerant of postmarital sex, people who abstain on the grounds of belief usually have some underlying emotional or sexual problem that makes them avoid sexual activity. They are critical of those who abstain because of religious beliefs and think that those beliefs may be a cover-up for some kind of serious inhibitions.

✎ **How do you feel about the paragraph you just read? Check your answer below.**

❏ Yes! I agree with this viewpoint.
❏ Angry. This is totally absurd.
❏ Confused. I am uncertain how I feel about this.
❏ Other _____

Divorced adults, even when incredible temptations face them, can be victorious through Christ.

This philosophy, which I naturally encountered early in my divorce, motivated me to write a Christian response which I called "A Part of Me Is Missing." But many people agree with this prevailing viewpoint and look at single adults who dare to say "no" or "NO!" as "strange" or as prime candidates for monkhood. Why do we need to be well-grounded in our convictions about how we respond sexually?

ONE: YOU ARE A SEXUAL PERSON. Sexuality is not what you do. Sexuality is what you are. Sexuality is all that it means to be male or female. Denying our sexual feelings and needs sets us up on the enemy's bull's-eye!

TWO: CHRISTIAN DIVORCED ADULTS ARE CALLED TO BE SALT AND LIGHT. Salt serves both as a preservative and as a seasoning. It combats decay and it flavors food. Light dispels darkness. In a dark and decaying world God intends for you to show people the way to "taste" and "see" godliness. If you lose your distinctive purity—your saltness—how will people know God? Salt that becomes mixed with impurities—that loses its saltness—is thrown out as garbage. We also are called to be light and hope to model another way to live one's life to resist sexually permissive societal attitudes. Here are some contemporary attitudes on sexual expression:

ATTITUDE 1: PERMISSIVE. This attitude is not difficult to memorize. Eight words summarize this philosophy of sexual hedonism.
• any time
• any place
• any one
• any thing.
"I've got to be me!" is the theme song. No wonder some people are addicted to sex. Their whole lives revolve around satisfying their sexual drives.

ATTITUDE 2: SELECTIVE. The phrase, "it depends . . ." summarizes many people's attitudes. To them, how they act sexually depends on—
• the situation: do I like this person?
• how I feel: do I love this person?
• whether I am sexually attracted to him/her.
• the status: we're in love.
• the fact that we're going together.
• the fact that we're going to be married.
• the risk: he's/she's not HIV+.
• that fact that no one will find out.
• the fact that my children are with my ex.
Those who are "selective" say, "I won't sleep with just anyone, but if the conditions are right, I might sleep with you."

Yes, you are missing out— on guilt, shame, a possible pregnancy, venereal diseases, and often a lot of regret.

ATTITUDE 3: DEPRIVATIONAL. The question, "What am I missing?" summarizes this attitude. For those with strong sexual drives or for those recently out of a marriage in which sex still was frequent, the sudden or forced adjustment to celibacy is not easy. Many people in this category settle for sex when what they really need is intimacy. Suspecting or knowing that our ex is sexually active heightens this attitude. To answer the question: Yes, you are missing out—on guilt, shame, a possible pregnancy, venereal disease, and often a lot of postsexual stress and regret.

ATTITUDE 4: FRUSTRATIONAL. Celibacy is not always fun. In fact, it can be downright frustrating—as is sleeping alone or eating alone. If you focus on the frustration, it only becomes more frustrating.

ATTITUDE 5: FRIGHTENED. The early days of divorce can be so overwhelming that some of us sink into a shell. Some of us are frightened by the dating world because we fear being rejected again.

 Do any of these attitudes apply to you? In the margin beside the five attitudes you just read, put a star by the attitude or attitudes that state how you feel now about sexual expression.

Bill Stearns in *Fine Lines* has offered the following wonderful set of statements that can help in making good sexual choices.

PRINCIPLES FOR DECISION MAKING

This choice of behavior or level of sexual expression is probably good if it—
• doesn't slow me down spiritually;
• can be profitable, useful;
• I can be Spirit-controlled in this;
• represents good stewardship of my body;
• doesn't violate my conscience (or my date's);
• I can value others through this;
• won't force a weaker brother/sister to violate his or her conscience;
• builds up fellow believers;
• demonstrates true Christianity to non-believers;
• can be done in submission to God's authority over me.[3]

I want to say "Yes!" to God's best.

Weekly Work

➠ **Repeat aloud the affirmation appearing at left.**

Discovering God's Wishes

In the affirmation you've stated, "I want to say 'Yes!' to God's best." For some of us, we may need to say, "I want to get to a place where I want to say or can say 'Yes!' to God's best." God's expectations are pretty clearly explained in His Word, which we will examine. In day 2 you learned about five attitudes about sexual expression. Here is the sixth and final one we still study:

ATTITUDE 6: BIBLICAL. A simple statement, "I will not seek or accept sexual expression contrary to biblical standards," summarizes this attitude.

DAY 3

Today's Objective:
I will discover God's wishes for my sexual expression.

✎ **If you adopted that attitude, which of the following would be acceptable, unacceptable, or questionable choices for sexual activity outside of marriage? Put a check under the statements that apply.**

	Acceptable	Unacceptable	Questionable
touching	❑	❑	❑
hugging	❑	❑	❑
light kissing	❑	❑	❑
French kissing	❑	❑	❑
fondling	❑	❑	❑
heavy petting	❑	❑	❑
oral sex	❑	❑	❑
stimulating partner to orgasm	❑	❑	❑
intercourse, no ejaculation	❑	❑	❑
intercourse	❑	❑	❑
just sleeping together (no sex)	❑	❑	❑

Everything is permissible for me—but not everything is beneficial . . . but I will not be mastered by anything. . . . The body is not meant for sexual immorality, but for the Lord.

–1 Corinthians 6:12-13

What this verse says to me—

_____

_____

_____

_____

Did you revert back to ATTITUDE 2: SELECTIVE to say, "Well, it depends"? Does it depend? On what? Read 1 Corinthians 6:12-13 appearing in the margin. In the margin box below the verse, describe what these words say to you.

You may have answered something like this: I will not do anything in regard to sexual expression that dishonors the Lord and that causes me to use my body in some way other than God's plan for sexuality. I will not make a choice that allows me to be tempted in a way that makes it impossible for me to honor Christ with my sexual expression.

Here are some Christ-honoring decisions that you can make about your sexual expression.

DECISION 1: I WILL NOT SEEK SEXUAL EXPRESSION CONTRARY TO BIBLICAL STANDARDS. It takes two to tango—two decision makers. Because we have been bought with a price, we never can use our sexuality to control, barter, manipulate, or exploit another. How could we do that and simultaneously "honor" God? We cannot, with integrity, try to override another person's "no."

Here are four Scriptures in which we find that biblical standard:
• 1 Corinthians 6:18: "Flee from sexual immorality."
• 1 Corinthians 6:20: "Therefore honor God with your body."
• 1 Timothy 5:1: "Treat younger men as brothers, older women as mothers, and younger women as sisters, with absolute purity."
• Titus 2:6: "Encourage the young men to be self-controlled."

✎ **What do these four Scriptures lead you to conclude is God's standard or desire for you?**

_____

In case you think Paul is prudish, listen to his own confession, "At one time we too were foolish, disobedient, deceived and enslaved by all kinds of passions and pleasures" (Titus 3:3). Notice his statement is past tense: "at one time we were . . .." How is that possible? Go back to Agenda 4 and look up

I am responsible for the degree of intimacy I seek or permit.

our memory verse. God isn't recruiting for a monastery where we can be shut away from all sexual temptation. Nor is He asking us to castrate ourselves as did the church father, Origen. He invites us to live, through the power of His Holy Spirit, in this present age.

Paul wrote young Timothy, "Train yourself to be godly" (1 Timothy 4:7). Paul used the word *train*. These incredible athletes who wow us in the Olympics do not just show up and announce, "I'm here. Which way is the locker room?" No, they train for years with incredible commitment to perform at a high competitive level. So, it is with sexuality. If we commit ourselves with an incredible commitment, if we train ourselves to resist temptation so we can honor God with our bodies, and if we rely on His strength rather than on ours, celibate we can be.

Think about the sexual choices you have made. Have they all been good, honorable, wise, or healthy? Maybe you've tried to keep God's standard but have failed—perhaps miserably. Maybe you need to talk to God.

➭ **Stop and pray this prayer:**
God, You know about/that _____

Sometimes we ask God to forgive specific acts, such as for sleeping with someone last month, rather than to forgive us for attitudes which precede the behavior. Talk to Him about your sexual attitudes, longings, desires, and frustrations:

God, I want You to forgive me for _____
God, I want You to help me with _____
God, help me not to seek sexual expression that is contrary to Your Word. Thank you. Amen.

DECISION 2: I WILL NOT ACCEPT SEXUAL EXPRESSION CONTRARY TO BIBLICAL STANDARDS. Accept. You might not seek sex, but what if someone offers it? Among the divorced, either male or female may be the initiator or sexual aggressor or sexual boundary challenger. Have you ever given in to sex because if you said no, he or she might think you are homosexual or weird or have a hang-up?

Linda told this story: "I became a Christian because of sex. I had a lot of anger toward men after my husband left me, so I slept around a lot—something I really regret. Then I met Mike—a great guy. He was different. A brilliant lawyer, he reminded me of the Southern gentleman—opening doors and all that. Well, after about four dates, when he still hadn't made a move, I just came right out and asked him, 'Are you gay or something?'

"'No!' he said. I think he was shocked. Then he said,'I can't sleep around because I am a Christian.' 'Well, so am I,' I said, 'I joined the church when I was seven.' 'Oh, no, it's more than that, ' he said. 'It's believing and living the way Christ wants me to live. It's not that I wouldn't want to have sex, but God calls me to a high standard.' Well, I looked at this guy like he was from the moon. 'Are you one of those 'born-again' freaks?' I asked.

Taking Jesus seriously

"'I am not a freak, but I do take Jesus seriously,'" he said. That word 'seriously' hit me like a ton of bricks. He wrote down some Scripture verses for me, but I didn't have a Bible, so I went to a bookstore and looked them up.

"'I called up his pastor and made an appointment with him. I told him what I've told you and something happened, there in his office. I prayed to accept Jesus. My friends freaked out when they heard what had happened. My life changed because I met two men who were not like other men I had known: Mike and his friend, Jesus. I am so glad Mike had some high standards."

A lot of people will offer sexual intimacy, especially if you have been hurt. They will volunteer to "help you" make it through, not only the night, but the divorce, as well.

✎ **Maybe you have not sought the sex but you did accept it. Below describe why you made this decision.**

_____

How has it turned out? _____

▀➡ **Maybe you clearly do not seek sex, but as a pattern, you will not say no. Maybe this is a time you need to talk to God. Stop and pray about this matter:**

God, you know about _____
God, I want You to forgive _____
God, I want You to help me _____
God, I want You to help me honor You with my body. Thank you. Amen.

Weekly Work

▀➡ **Say aloud three times this week's memory verse.**

▀➡ **Repeat aloud the affirmation appearing at left.**

Recognizing Temptation

Diplomats know that "hot spots," or mini-wars, that break out in sometimes isolated spots on the globe cannot be ignored because these hot spots have ways of evolving into larger, perhaps global conflicts. The same is true of sexual "hot spots." Little sexual temptations we might consider harmless have a way of escalating. Before long you may be asking yourself, "Has God really said no sex outside of marriage?"

A little boy once found a bear cub and decided to keep it in the smokehouse as a pet. He kept feeding the cub, but soon it was a bear—eventually a big bear that vastly complicated the boy's life. Maybe you have some "cub" sexual thoughts or behaviors. How long will they remain in the cub stage?

Motivations for Sexual Expression

Here are some things that can motivate us in choosing the way we express ourselves sexually:

I want to say "Yes!" to God's best.

DAY 4

Today's objective:
I will learn to recognize the "hot spots" of sexual temptation for divorced adults.

1. Sexual expression can be faith-based. Some divorced people decide, "I intend to live my life with sexual integrity. Therefore, I must say 'no' to any sexual invitations that compromise my faith."

2. Sexual expression can be curiosity-based. As single adults with ears and eyes, we hear and read about the sexual mores of the divorced, especially the myth of the "swinging" single. Some who have lived in a marriage with poor sexual relations may be curious about what sex could be like. Those who have had no sex or bad sex in a marriage may feel deprived.

3. Sexual expression can be anger-based. One of the most beautiful women I ever met was divorced. "Who in their right mind would divorce you?" I asked her. "He left me for my best friend," she answered. Then she told her reaction: In her anger, she slept with as many men as possible.

4. Sexual expression can be "moment"-based. These individuals have been so wounded, they have little hope for a better tomorrow. "Grab all the gusto now" is their motto. Unfortunately they compromise tomorrow on the altar of today. Celibacy is decided not once and for all; for most of us, it's moment by moment. A choice in a weak moment today could complicate your tomorrow.

Complicating tomorrows

5. Sexual expression can be "panic"-based. Many divorced people use sex to hang onto people; men can be pretty callous in noting, "Look around. A lot of women are out there." Or as one man told a friend of mine, "Here's my number. Call me when you change your mind about having sex." Fortunately, she never called him. A person can panic and say, "I'll never meet anyone," and with that reasoning can say "yeses" that come back to haunt.

6. Some divorced people live their lives captive to their emotions and feelings. Volunteers abound who want to "cheer you up" sexually. Sex, in this instance, is an anesthetic; it feels good at the moment. But like all anesthesia, the good feeling wears off, and you have new pain to deal with.

In the space below check the "base" that influences your sexual expression.
- ❏ faith-based
- ❏ curiosity-based
- ❏ anger-based
- ❏ moment-based
- ❏ panic-based
- ❏ emotion-based

Why does this "base" work for you? _____

Outlets for Sexual Expression

No shortages of sexual discount "outlets" exist. Stand in a grocery-store line and scan the magazine headlines. Or tune in to your favorite afternoon talk show and listen to some of the sexually explicit topics discussed. Unfortunately, we take in a lot of sex-related stimulation: movies, music lyrics, television themes, reading, and process all these in our own lives.

Sadly, even some of our friends tease us or mock us for our sexual decisions. They say, "You're such a prude!" "How are you ever going to meet someone when you are so uptight!?" We initially may laugh, but later we re-play those remarks, perhaps in slow motion, and we question our own sexual values.

Most divorced people don't just wake up one morning and say, "I wonder how many of the Ten Commandments I can break by midnight!" Sexual sin starts with sexual ideas—thoughts that they toy with.

Agenda 5 addressed the issue of guarding your heart. Remember those toothpaste commercials by a certain toothpaste hawking its "invisible shield" which prevented tooth decay? Well, some of our far-too-fragile-not-yet-fully-healed hearts need an "invisible shield" of protection.

And the peace of God, which transcends all understanding, will guard your hearts and minds in Christ Jesus.

–Philippians 4:7

Also, guard your minds. Paul, who as a single adult could have had some battles with sexual temptation, offered some seasoned advice in Philippians 4:7, which appears at left. I am not sure that Paul had to deal with the sex-saturation of our culture—although Corinth was no Mayberry, R.F.D.—but he did know the power of thoughts to precede actions. He advised us to think about whatever is true, whatever is noble, whatever is right, whatever is pure, whatever is admirable, whatever is excellent or praiseworthy.

 To show how our culture works to plant sexual standards that challenge our faith and our "no's" through movies, books, films, television, celebrity lives, let's do a scorecard. Think about a movie, a television show, and a book you've seen or read recently. Write in the titles and then ask yourself how many of the above criteria were met. Put a check in the appropriate categories.

Movie Title	TV Show Title	Book Title
_____	_____	_____
❑ true	❑ true	❑ true
❑ noble	❑ noble	❑ noble
❑ right	❑ right	❑ right
❑ pure	❑ pure	❑ pure
❑ admirable	❑ admirable	❑ admirable
❑ excellent	❑ excellent	❑ excellent
❑ praiseworthy	❑ praiseworthy	❑ praiseworthy
❑ edified God	❑ edified God	❑ edified God
❑ helped me	❑ helped me	❑ helped me

A progression occurs, especially on sleepless nights when you toss and turn. Little thoughts such as those below keep darting into our minds.

Thought invaders

- Thought invader 1: You know you don't have to be sleeping alone.
- Thought invader 2: _____ is a Christian and is not sleeping alone.
- Thought invader 3: You know the Bible was written a long, long time ago.
- Thought invader 4: Did God really mean no sex?
- Thought invader 5: Your ex's new honey—she's gorgeous! I bet they're not celibate!
- Thought invader 6: You're so young . . . too bad you're never going to have sex again!

In Psalm 10:4 the psalmist comments on the wicked, "in all his thoughts there is no room for God." You're not wicked, but in your night thoughts, in your tossing and turning, do you have "room for God?"

✎ **How can I make "room for God" in my thoughts, especially at night? Below write your answer.**

1. By _____
2. By _____
3. By _____
4. By _____
5. By _____

You may have written something like this: I will make room for God by not reading or viewing material that does not reflect the way He intends for us to act sexually. I will make room for God by spending some time before I go to bed reflecting on His love for me and thanking Him for the blessings in my life.

▶ **Stop and pray. Voice aloud the following prayer:**
O God, you made sexual expression. You designed us with such an intricate sexual system. You endowed us with such powerful longings and the thrill of being touched. Help us as divorced individuals to "honor" You. Help us to know that we are not abnormal even though we live in such a sexually-saturated culture. Teach us to say no even when our bodies want to say yes. Especially help us in our night season, when the thought invaders come in waves. Remind us that You want to help us. Amen.

Weekly Work

▶ **Reflect on the memory verse, slightly adapted to today's lesson.**
"Do I know that my body—this body—is a temple of the Holy Spirit?"
"Do I know that the Holy Spirit is in me?"
"Do I know that I have received the Holy Spirit from God, as a gift?"
"Do I understand that I am not my own?"
"Do I appreciate the great price God bought me with?"
"Am I willing—really willing—to honor God with my body—this body?

▶ **Repeat aloud the affirmation appearing at left.**

*If I am to say "Yes!"
to God's best,
I will have to guard my
heart and my mind.*

DAY 5

Today's objective:
I will learn my personal "no" boundaries.

Knowing My "No" Strategies

Maybe some divorced people would be better off if we occasionally mimicked two-year-olds who seem to be obsessed with "no." At times that is the only word in their vocabulary. Among the divorced, many of us have only one word, possibly two, in our vocabularies—yes and maybe—at least when sexual expression is concerned.

All of us need to practice our "no" skills. On a few occasions, a fast-talking sales clerk sold me something not only that I did not need but that I did not even want. These days, particularly in the arena of sexual expression, divorced people need to practice their "no" skills to avoid sexual "hucksters" and gunslingers. Look at the word KNOW: K-N-O-W. Look closely. What do you see? N-O. Some of us need to know some "no" skills. Consider these:

GUIDELINE #1: KNOW YOUR DATES. Any time you go to bed with someone, you are going to bed with every sexual partner that person has had in the last seven years, according to former Surgeon General C. Everett Koop.5 That means that some people won't be able to get the bedroom door closed because of all the people with whom they previously have had sex and every person that person has had sex with.

Many people meet others through the classifieds. Some people seem very naive in answering the ads. Can you believe everything he/she tells you? How many times has he/she been married? Was his/her ex as bad as described? Are you certain this person is as innocent as he/she claims? Are alimony and child-support payments up to date? Where you look has a lot to do with what you find.

GUIDELINE #2: KNOW YOUR OWN SEXUAL THRESHOLD. Once you have been accustomed to sex in a marriage, in all probability, holding hands is not going to be a big turn on. Besides, some of us did not particularly care for Adolescence I, so the prospects of a prolonged Adolescence II is not exciting. Know your own sexual boundaries—boundaries you will not compromise.

Know your own sexual boundaries—boundaries you will not compromise.

Steve Arterburn, a seasoned counselor, once advised a single who worried that she didn't date because something was wrong with her, "I don't think the reason you are single is because there is something wrong in your life. I think you are single because of something right in your life. Through your unwillingness to have sex before marriage you have essentially eliminated 75 percent of the dating pool—even in the church community."[2]

GUIDELINE #3: BE CONSISTENT WITH YOUR NO'S. No today/yes tomorrow confuses a lot of people. When people are in a good place with God, they are more likely to say "no," but when their quiet time is lacking, their "no's" also may be lacking.

When people are in a good place with God, they are more likely to say "no."

GUIDELINE #4: SAY NO QUICKLY, DIRECTLY, FIRMLY AND CALMLY. Many people have difficulty understanding that "no" to sex means "no." Sometimes a person can couch the "no" in such a way that it can send conflicting signals which lead the person to assume, "She is just playing hard to get" or "If she says yes, she thinks I'll think she's easy."

GUIDELINES #5: WARN BEFORE THE NO ZONE. Tell your dates up front—no sex. You may have heard the salesperson's creed, "Salesmanship doesn't even begin until the customer says 'no.'" That's the way some divorced people operate in trying to talk another into having sex. Sometimes people think "no" means, a little more persuasion." Take preventative action to avoid situations that compromise or challenge our ability to say "no."

GUIDELINE #6: LET THE NEEDLE GET STUCK ON "NO." Ever heard a record get stuck and the same phrase keeps getting repeated? Use the broken-record approach. No. No. No. No.

GUIDELINE #7: DON'T BE BADGERED OR BELITTLED. Although grown men seldom say "pretty please" in sex, they come close. No one has the right to try to override another's "no." If a man or woman keeps pushing for a level of sex with which you are uncomfortable, that is a sure indication that he/she could not possibly be the right one for you.

GUIDELINE #8: REHEARSE YOUR NO. I have learned that I have to rehearse my "no" before I arrive in the restaurant. The server may say, "Would you like to see our dessert tray?" which translated means, "Wouldn't you like to spend more money so my tip will be larger?" I have learned that a "no" at that point is easier than a "no" once the dessert tray is on the table.

GUIDELINE #9: EXPLAIN YOUR REASONING. Some folks think your "no" is a "no" to them, so it stings. Some people use sex to prop up a bruised self-image. "Don't you find me attractive?" they might ask. Turn back to page 122 and reread Linda's story. Michael, her date, was able to explain his "no" in a straightforward manner.

✎ **Read 1 Peter 3:15 appearing in the margin. In the box below it write the verse in your own words. Translate it into contemporary language as it deals with sexual temptation and celibacy.**

In 1 Timothy 4:16, Paul wrote Timothy some words that need to be heard by single adults today: "Watch your life and doctrine closely." By this point in their lives many single adults may have their doctrinal beliefs pretty settled. But often, too often, our lives and our lifestyle and sexual choices are in direct conflict with what we say we believe.

GUIDELINE #10: ANTICIPATE THE WANT-TO BLUES AFTER A "NO." Our bodies have a difficult time reconciling reality with the current moment. Physiologically, during marriage, they were accustomed to sexual response and release. It's almost like launching the space shuttle; the conditions are similar, but a "hold" occurs on launch. Missions have to be "scrubbed." Your body may be asking, "What's going on?"

If you have been accustomed to an active sex life, in marriage or outside of marriage, abstinence can be a tough experience. It's like your body is saying, "Whoa! Who changed the rules?" Nothing is wrong with you if you miss intercourse. What is wrong is the way we deal with what we miss.

GUIDELINE #11: "NO" CAN RESULT IN PAIN. Sometimes "no" has consequences. He/she never calls us again—and "good riddance" doesn't cut it. It hurts.

Steve Arterburn writes: "In this country it is extremely difficult to be single and adhere to sexual abstinence. Adhering to your Christian values may cost you something rather than get you something. Some singles get very angry when they hear this message. But the truth is that peace will only come when we can reach a point where—mate or no mate—we can say, 'I'm yours, Lord. You don't need to deliver to me _____ (fill in the blank) to prove that you love me.'"[12]

What if the he or she to whom you said "no" starts dating someone you know or someone in your single-adult fellowship? That may be awkward and painful, but not nearly as painful as the results of compromising your sexual and emotional integrity.

GUIDELINE #12: GOD THINKS "NO" IS A GOOD IDEA. This guideline's reality is like the foundation that supports a building or the bedrock. Some divorced people want it spelled out for them. To answer the enemy's question, "Has God really said no?", read 1 Thessalonians 4:3-6 appearing in the

Always be prepared to give an answer to everyone who asks you to give the reason for the hope you have.

–1 Peter 3:15

What this verse means to me—

_____

_____

_____

_____

What if good riddance hurts?

It is God's will that you should be holy; that you should avoid sexual immorality; that each of you should learn to control his body in a way that is holy and honorable, not in passionate lust like the heathen, who do not know God; and that in this matter no one should wrong his brother [or sister] or take advantage of him [or her].

–1 Thessalonians 4:3-6

I am going to have to say "no" often in order to say "YES!" to God's best.

margin. That verse is pretty clear. Perhaps you've seen the T-shirt which reads, "Which part of no don't you understand?"

➠ **Say aloud the following prayer:**
God, "no" has not been an exhausted word in my vocabulary. But I want to learn to say no. I want to honor You with my body. I want to live my life as a divorced person with sexual and emotional integrity. So, this moment, I ask You to help me. Teach me, through Your grace, to say no.

Weekly Work

✎ **Write in the margin this week's memory verse.**

➠ **Repeat aloud the affirmation appearing in the margin.**

Notes
[1]Bill Stearns, *Fine Lines*, (San Bernardino: Here's Life Publishers, 1987), 146.
[2]"Conversation with Stephen Arterburn." SAM JOURNAL (Issue #101 & 102), 16.
[3]Ibid.

AGENDA
9

This week's agenda:
You will understand the biblical perspective on divorce and remarriage.

Some Biblical Dimensions

BEFORE THE "I-DO" DECISION

Beth and David met while each was going through divorce; mutual friends introduced them. Beth's husband left her for a friend, and Beth inherited most of the bills. She is a single parent with two children: ages three and five. The boys are a handful, and her ex rarely comes up with any money for her and the boys. David has four grown children; his marriage ended after 22 years.

David never has been much of a church person; Beth has been active in her local church but has been reluctant to tell anyone in the church about her relationship with David for fear people will not approve.

What are some matters that Beth and David should consider before they enter into marriage? This unit addresses, from a biblical perspective, situations like Beth and David's.

What you will learn

This week you will—
- confront the reality of divorce and remarriage;
- examine the grounds for remarriage;
- grapple with key questions you need to answer before you consider the "I-do" decision;
- distinguish between grace, law, and license;
- consider your commitment to the best.

What you will study

Confronting the Reality	Examining the Grounds	Examining the Grounds, Part II	Before You Say "I Do" 2	Asking the Right Questions
DAY 1	DAY 2	DAY 3	DAY 4	DAY 5

Memory verse

This week's verse of Scripture to memorize—
I [Jesus] have come that they may have life, and have it to the full.

—John 10:10

Confronting the Reality

Today's objective:
I will confront the fact that divorce and remarriage are realities in our society and in the church.

Some statistics to ponder

Divorce has reached epidemic proportions in our society, and Christians are not immune. According to Richard Fowler of the Minirth-Meier Counseling Clinic, the divorce rate for Christians is only 10 percent below that for non-Christians.

Because of the American commitment to "a second chance," people naturally find themselves remarrying. Indeed, some worry that most Americans are skeptical about the success of first marriages. The average marriage ended by divorce is only 7.1 years long, typified by the stereotypical "seven-year itch." Divorce happens, and remarriage happens as well.

Statistically: 75 percent of males will remarry within 14 months of the divorce; a significant percentage will live with someone of the opposite sex as either a transition from the previous marriage and/or into the next marriage. Lenore J. Weitzman notes, "The likelihood of a woman's remarriage is largely a function of her age at the time of divorce."[1] When a woman is between 30 and 40, she is as likely to remain single as to marry again; however, if she is over 40, she probably will not marry again. Whether she marries or not, she is likely to spend a number of years alone as a single parent. Since few divorced women immediately remarry, and given the significant decline in alimony awarded to women, many will be financially strapped.

Increasingly judges see remarriage by the woman as an "alternative" to the stereotypical female, financially strapped single parent; many conclude it is preferable to "saddling her former husband with the responsibility for her support."[2] Increasingly, alimony is a rarity in divorce settlements, or it has a cut-off date—say two years.

Indeed, this is one reality in the "stats" approach that is troublesome; some of these are multiple divorces. In 1988 (the last year complete stats were available) in almost half of the marriages, one partner had been married previously; in almost one-quarter both had been married before.

We benefit when we remember that each of these stats is a person—a human being with feelings, emotions, tears, and a heart. We have become so statistically-oriented that we fail to sense the pain behind the statistics.

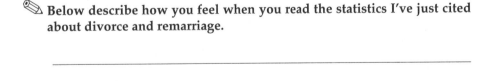 **Below describe how you feel when you read the statistics I've just cited about divorce and remarriage.**

_____

_____

You may have responded that you feel sad because you now find yourself as one of the statistics that I just mentioned. You may have said that you felt comforted to realize so many other people are in the same boat you are: contemplating whether starting over in a new marriage is the right thing for them. Regardless of your answer, we can't deny these statistics. In this week's agenda we'll discuss the biblical foundations which serve as a baseline for any considerations of divorce and remarriage.

DAY 2

Today's objective:
I will examine the grounds for divorce and/or remarriage.

Confronting the question

Weekly Work

 Begin to memorize this week's memory verse, John 10:10. Say it aloud three times.

➡ Repeat the affirmation appearing at left.

Examining the Grounds

Few issues in the Christian community can generate more debate than can contemplating the grounds for divorce and/or remarriage. For many people the issue is simple to debate because it is abstract; however, when a particular face or name becomes part of the issue, many head back to Scripture for another look.

Our discussion begins with this question: "What has God really said and what has He really not said?"

Read this quote from H. Wayne House: "Unfortunately, there is no universal agreement in the evangelical community regarding what the Bible teaches about divorce. Even among godly and scholarly theologians and pastors, there is a diversity of opinion on the meaning and application of the biblical teaching in this area. Even so, we need to determine in our own minds what Scripture teaches on the subject so that we may have a clear conscience before God as we confront the question or give counsel to others."[3]

✎ **What do you believe are the biblical grounds for divorce and remarriage? Write the answer below.**

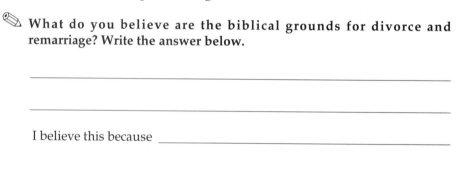

_____

_____

I believe this because _____

_____

House summarizes the biblical background on marriage this way:
1. God instituted marriage.
2. Marriage requires making a new and public commitment.
3. In marriage the man and woman become one flesh.
4. It was the symbol of Yahweh's covenant with Israel.
5. Jesus had great respect for the marriage union. He used weddings or marriage as the subject of several of His parables.
6. It is used to illustrate the relationship between Christ and the church.[4]

Marriage is a monogamous relationship in which a man and woman share a lifetime commitment to glorify God through growth in oneness. Marriage is a relationship of responsible love in which the commitment of the couple to each other is second only to their commitment to God. It is an unconditional, lifetime commitment. Jesus emphasized that marriage be a lifelong commitment.[5]

This definition highlights these three key features of marriage:
1. commitment to spouse second only to God
2. unconditional
3. for life

Here are some basics to consider about the biblical background of divorce and remarriage:

1. Both divorce and remarriage existed in the Old Testament period. Indeed, "divorce was understood to be a doorway to remarriage. In fact, the very idea of 'divorce' was such that remarriage was expected!"[6] Old Testament Law established that a man (no mention of a woman divorcing her husband) give his wife a certificate of divorce, as the first part of Deuteronomy 24:1-4 appearing at left indicates. One scholar writes, "Without the divorce certificate, another man could be charged with stealing or violating the property rights of the first husband, should he take the woman as wife or servant. Thus the writing of divorce was intended to place some limits upon the husband and to afford the wife some protection.[7]

> If a man marries a woman who becomes displeasing to him because he finds something indecent about her, and he writes her a certificate of divorce, gives it to her and sends her from his house, and if after she leaves his house she becomes the wife of another man, and her second husband dislikes her and writes her a certificate of divorce, gives it to her and sends her from his house, or if he dies, then her first husband, who divorced her, is not allowed to marry her again after she has been defiled. That would be detestable in the eyes of the Lord.
>
> –Deuteronomy 24:1-4

For women, little economic alternative to remarriage—other than prostitution—existed in that day. A woman of that era needed a man's protection. Also, because the Jews were expected to be as numerous as the "stars of the sky," every male was expected to remarry to continue to have children.

2. God hates divorce. Read what the Bible says in Malachi 2:16, appearing at left. Few verses have been used as strongly in portraying God's opposition to divorce as has this one in Malachi.

> "For I hate divorce," says the Lord God of Israel, "and covering one's garment with violence," says the Lord of hosts.
>
> –Malachi 2:16,RSV

✎ **How do you feel when you read this verse? Below write your answer.**

Whenever I hear that verse, I feel _____

I feel this way because _____

One of the basic rules of Scripture interpretation is to examine the setting in which the words are spoken. In this period—five centuries before Jesus—the Jews commonly abandoned their Jewish wives (especially older wives) and married unbelieving Gentile women. Again, many rationalized the process as giving them a chance for more offspring.

We generally put a period in this passage where God only put a comma. Look back at the rest of Malachi 2:16 to the portion seldom quoted. T. Miles Bennett in the *Broadman Bible Commentary* explains that "covering one's garment with violence" was to "act in a violent and unjust manner toward one's wife or the marriage relationship."[8] This has implications in an era of spousal physical abuse. God hates divorce. He also hates violence in the marriage relationship.

Divorce and remarriage in Jesus' day

At the time Jesus began His public ministry, Jews were divided into two camps on the issue of divorce. One group followed the rabbi Shammai and the others supported the interpretations of rabbi Hillel. Their arguments focused on Deuteronomy 24:1, which assumed the practice of divorce but attempted to regulate it. The debate between the learned rabbis and their followers narrowed down to how they interpreted the phrase, "something indecent" or literally "the nakedness of a thing . . ."

Shammai and Company stressed the word *nakedness*—divorce permissible only on the grounds of a wife's adultery. Hillel and Company stressed the word *something*—divorce permissible on any grounds, including "the wife's burning of the husband's food, or the husband's seeing a woman who pleased him better."[9]

So, we arrive at Matthew 19:3-12, which begins, "Some Pharisees came to him to test him." See the Scripture appearing at left.

> Some Pharisees came to him to test him. They asked, "Is it lawful for a man to divorce his wife for any and every reason?"
>
> –Matthew 19:3

✎ **What do we know about the Pharisees? What was their motivation in inquiring of Jesus? Check the answers below that apply.**

❑ A. to find out what Jesus believed about divorce
❑ B. to drag Jesus into the debate between the followers of Shammai and Hillel, knowing for him to side with one group would irritate the others
❑ C. to trick him
❑ D. to embarrass him; after all, he had never been married

The Pharisees' questions of Jesus were not sincere: the Pharisees were not engaged in an intellectual discussion just to enrich their minds. They clearly hoped to trap Jesus into taking sides in their controversy. The correct answers were statements B and C. Let's examine the loaded questions they asked to trick Him.

LOADED QUESTION ONE: "Is it lawful for a man to divorce his wife for any and every reason?" The Pharisees prided themselves on adhering to the Law–even to outrageous points. They ask, "Is it permissible?" However, they gave themselves away by the words *for any and every reason*. We have to assume a crowd heard the discussion and that the crowd must have contained a few remarried men who had divorced their wives for flimsy reasons.

> "Haven't you read," he replied, "that at the beginning the Creator 'made them male and female,' and said, 'For this reason a man will leave his father and mother and be united with his wife, and the two will become one flesh'? So they are no longer two, but one. Therefore what God has joined together, let man not separate."
>
> –Matthew 19:4-6

> "Why then," they asked, "did Moses command that a man give his wife a certificate of divorce and send her away?" Jesus replied, "Moses permitted you to divorce your wives because your hearts were hard. But it was not this way from the beginning."
>
> –Matthew 19:7-8

What does Jesus do? He sidesteps the question. Jesus did not speak to the issue of divorce but of marriage and God's intentions: the two become one flesh (19:5). Jesus sums it up with, "Therefore what God has joined together, let man not separate" (v. 6). *End of discussion*, so it seemed, but the Pharisees had an "itching-for-an argument" mentality.

LOADED QUESTION TWO: "Why then did Moses command that a man give his wife a certificate of divorce and send her away?" was their next question. (See the verses appearing at left.) Remember in Agenda 8, Day 1, how the enemy toyed with the words, "You must not eat . . . of any tree in the Garden?" The Pharisees did the same thing. They had switched the words for their advantage. The Pharisees said, "Moses commanded"; Jesus said, "Moses permitted." Big difference between what is commanded and what is permitted! But Jesus continued, "because your hearts were hard" (v. 8).

One commentator writes, "Even 'lawful' divorce is a violation of God's ideal will, and thus in essence is sin . . . .. When Jesus stated this position, the Pharisees were stunned . . . .. God permitted divorce 'for the hardness of your hearts.' That is, God made provision in His law for the impact of sin on human nature. . . .. Marriage was instituted prior to the entry of sin, and a permanent union remains God's ideal for humankind. But when sin entered with the first couple's disobedience, our experience of the ideal was shattered. What became real was that human hearts are hard."[10]

Remember, in this period, no courts existed to mediate the divorce. The husband merely could say, "This marriage is over." Too bad if the wife was cheated or inconvenienced or did not agree. The man's assessment was final.

The Pharisees must have been squirming because Jesus hammered them with a conviction they could not have possibly expected. He said, "I tell you that anyone who divorces his wife, except for marital unfaithfulness, and marries another woman commits adultery." To the Pharisees, who tried to get him to choose between two schools of thought, His "anyone" meant either school.

Jesus did not mince words. But that sentence has been highly scrutinized and debated, particularly the words between the two commas. Many argue that this clause does not appear in Mark 10:11-12 or in Luke 16:18–other biblical references to this topic–and therefore is suspect. House sums up the attitude of many when he says, "Since marriage is not constituted solely on the sexual union, it is inconsistent to say that it is dissolved solely on the basis of sexual infidelity."[11] Some go so far as to argue that the syntax of the exception clause links it to the divorce rather than remarriage. Thus, they would argue that a person can get a divorce—particularly for adultery—but cannot remarry.[12]

In the next segment we'll continue to look at biblical perspective on divorce and remarriage.

> I tell you that anyone who divorces his wife, except for marital unfaithfulness, and marries another woman commits adultery.
>
> –Matthew 19:9

I am learning that the tragedies of life can fertilize tomorrow's dream because I am an M.I.P. (miracle-in-progress).

DAY 3

Today's objective:
I will continue to examine the grounds for divorce and remarriage.

Weekly Work

✎ Write in the margin three times our memory verse for the week.

⏭ Repeat the affirmation appearing at left.

Examining the Grounds, Part II

Let's look at some more things we can learn from Scripture on the matter of divorce and remarriage.

1. Scripture does not condemn all divorce. John Splinter, who has worked with thousands of Christians after divorce, raises the issue of God's demand that 113 Israelite men divorce their foreign wives, as portrayed in Ezra 10:11, which reads, "Now make confession to the Lord, the God of your fathers, and do his will. Separate yourselves from the peoples around you and from your foreign wives." Splinter says, "The point is that if God were totally and universally opposed to divorce, He would not have commanded 113 men to divorce their wives. Yet, even in this text, divorce is seen to exist within a painful and difficult situation."[13] Moreover, it is not insignificant that these 113 men had names and that many were leaders in Israel.

2. Remarriage may occur when the divorce resulted from adultery. House says, "Jesus gave a general principle, 'a married couple should not divorce'" and adds that the verse may be paraphrased, "Unless one's spouse has been unfaithful, to divorce and remarry is to commit adultery."[14]

House states, "the word translated 'marital unfaithfulness' in the NIV is a general word which covers all kinds of sexual immorality: homosexual relations, incest, and adultery. When one marriage partner breaks the sexual bond, the other partner may (key word is may) end the relationship."[15] This would especially be the case, many would argue, when systematic, long-term adultery or sexual unfaithfulness has occurred—what Zuck and Walvoord label a "relentless, persistent, unrepentant lifestyle of sexual unfaithfulness."[16]

One incident of unfaithfulness would not necessarily be adequate grounds for divorce; it could be grounds for forgiveness. However, some wronged partners—because of the hardness of their hearts—have seized the incident and headed for a divorce lawyer, as they wrap themselves in biblical "cause" or grounds.

One act of sexual unfaithfulness could expose that person's spouse to a potentially fatal illness.

However, in today's world—given the reality of AIDS, herpes, and other sexually transmitted diseases, a person's one act of sexual unfaithfulness could expose his or her spouse to a potentially fatal or incurable illness. The stakes indeed are high.

But if the unbeliever leaves, let him do so. A believing man or woman is not bound in such circumstances; God has called us to live in peace.

–1 Corinthians 7:15

3. Remarriage may occur when an unbelieving spouse departs. Read 1 Corinthians 7:15 appearing in the margin. Is a believing spouse to fight a divorce at all costs? In an era of epidemic family abuse, staying together at all costs could mean being shot or killed. If the unbelieving partner leaves (depart is the biblical word, a common word for divorce in the ancient world), the believing partner no longer is bound "to a marriage that no longer exists,"[17] writes House.

But what if a believer "departs"—moves out of the home—as happens commonly in today's era of "no-fault" divorce? Some people would argue the same line of logic as a departure by an unbelieving spouse. Your options may be more limited in what you can do.
• You may be able to do little to prevent the divorce if your spouse wants it;
• If the believer who departs remarries, then by the standards of Matthew 19:9, he/she has committed adultery; that type of unfaithfulness frees the spouse to remarry.

Many consider desertion to be the same thing as sexual unfaithfulness, since the party who deserted has broken the marriage covenant. At some point, he/she likely will—given the statistics of sexual behavior among the separated/divorced—have sex and thus commit adultery.

Moreover, some people advance this argument: We must understand the spirit of Scripture. If a man is intravenously doing drugs and sharing needles, he/she is being exposed to AIDS and is transferring that exposure to an innocent party. Surely, Paul would not say because no adultery/desertion occurs a spouse is bound to him/her.

God does not want His people to be divorced, but He does know that unrepentant adultery and desertion occur in a fallen world. Since God does not zap the survivor of these situations into physiological celibacy, He allows remarriage after divorce.

Remarriage after widowhood clearly was permissible in the New Testament Church (Romans 7:2-3, appearing on the next page). In fact, Paul counseled young widows to remarry because "when their sensual desires (their sexual

For example, by law a married woman is bound to her husband as long as he is alive, but if her husband dies, she is released from the law of marriage. So then, if she marries another man while her husband is still alive, she is called an adulteress. But if her husband dies, she is released from that law and is not an adulteress, even though she marries another man.

–Romans 7:2-3

drive) overcome their dedication to Christ, they want to marry"(1 Timothy 5:11). Paul made some concessions to the power of the sex drive.

However, Paul added a stipulation to widows, "She is free to marry anyone she wishes, but he must belong to the Lord" or be a Christian (1 Corinthians 7:39). That is wise counsel for those who have been divorced. Even when divorce and desertion are present—and accepted as grounds for divorce/remarriage—these persons still are to marry someone "in the Lord."

✎ **Do you believe that Paul's stipulation that widows marry only believers is good advice for divorced individuals considering remarriage? Below explain your answer.**

_____

_____

_____

_____

The Option of Singleness

Scripture also is positive about the fact that people have a choice of remaining single and not remarrying. In our culture many people assume that you must marry to be a complete person. Scripture presents a very different view. The Bible not only makes clear that we have an option of remaining single, it even suggests that singleness is the most ideal lifestyle. To those who are unmarried the apostle Paul said, "It is good for them to stay unmarried, as I am. If they cannot control themselves, they should marry, for it is better to marry than to burn with passion" (1 Corinthians 7:8-9).

For some are eunuchs because they were born that way; others were made that way by men; and others have renounced marriage because of the kingdom of heaven. The one who can accept this should accept it.

Matthew 19:12

As you make decisions about remarriage, remember that Jesus affirmed people who remain single for the purpose of serving God. In Matthew 19:12 he said that some were physical eunuchs, and some people choose celibacy because of their spiritual commitment. (See the verse appearing in the margin and also see 1 Corinthians 7:11 appearing in the margin on page 140.) Remaining single allows an individual to serve God without dividing loyalties between God and his or her mate.

Good Words for Wounded People

The woman said to him, "Sir, give me this water so that I won't get thirsty and have to keep coming here to draw water." He told her, "Go, call your husband and come back." "I have no husband," she replied.

–John 4:15-17

The good news often ignored in studying these matters is a powerful exchange that took place at a well in Samaria. Jesus, alone, dared, as a Jew, to ask a Samaritan woman for a drink. She was stunned: "You are a Jew . . .. How can you ask me for a drink?" At this time, Jews thought Samaritans were scum. After the initial bantering back and forth, Jesus says, "Whoever drinks the water I give him will never thirst" (John 4:14). Read the verse at left to see what happens next.

Jesus then says to her, "You are right when you say you have no husband." Jesus bulls-eyed her! Before she could answer, He adds, "You have had five husbands, and the man you now have is not your husband. What you have

If God could see a future for the Samaritan woman who turned to Him, He can see a future for me!

Many of the Samaritans from that town believed in him because of the woman's testimony.

–John 4:39

just said is quite true." She tries to get away by asking a theological question that is not relevant to the discussion, but Jesus bulls-eyed her a second time when He says, "I am the Messiah." Jesus recognized her five marriages as a reality. He could have said, "You have one husband and four pseudo-husbands." But He recognized the marriages as well as their impact on her. He does not condone her lifestyle, but He signifies that she has worth. By following Him, she became a valued part of the Kingdom of God.

As we see, this woman is not to be forgotten; she became the first soul-winner in the early church. If you have difficulty believing this, read John 4:39 appearing in the margin to see how Scripture describes what happened. We will have neighbors in heaven who came to Christ through the witness of a woman who had five husbands, whose life in the future was governed by her encounter with Christ when she followed Him. Jesus didn't change her marital past, but He did change her heart for the future. As one who turned to Jesus, she still could be useful to Christ despite what she had done in her past.

 Check the statements below that you believe apply to you:

When I read the story of the Samaritan woman I feel–
- ❏ hopeless; God could never use me because of the things that have happened in my life
- ❏ devastated; God may have forgiven the Samaritan woman but He never could forgive me
- ❏ hopeful; I can accept God's forgiveness because I've turned my life over to Him
- ❏ optimistic; perhaps God is not sitting in judgment of me after all since I repented
- ❏ other _____

Christians have a tendency to want to legalize grace rather than bask in the outrageous mercy of a God who cares enough to reach out and heal sinful people who turn to Him.

Weekly Work

✎ **In the margin write what this week's memory verse means to you.**

➠ **Repeat the affirmation appearing at left.**

I am learning that the tragedies of life can fertilize tomorrow's dream because I am an M.I.P. (miracle-in-progress).

DAY 4

Today's objective:
I will grapple with important questions before I consider an "I do."

Before You Say "I Do" 2

James and Maryo planned to marry in Las Vegas. Only one thing stood between them and the "I do": a cardboard box containing the ashes of James' first wife. They had planned to scatter her ashes in the Grand Canyon to dramatically symbolize the end of his first marriage. However, thieves broke into James' car and made off with "Judy." A distraught James explained, "I don't see how we can be married now until we get Judy taken care of."[18]

Thousands of couples anticipating remarriage find themselves in James and Maryo's dilemma. Physical ashes don't hinder them, but emotional ashes do.

Unfinished business. Perhaps a hostile ex or children. Too many ties to the past. Too many matters unsettled.

Paul Giblin, who has trained many pastoral counselors, urges counselors as well as friends and family to take more seriously what we dismiss as premarital "jitters." Giblin argues that people routinely should ask couples planning to remarry, "Could this relationship ever be called off, and if so, what would the grounds be?"

Even when people believe they are free under the Scriptures to remarry, remarriage may be wrong for them if certain matters in their lives are not taken care of. They can consider these questions.

QUESTION 1: HAVE I FORGIVEN MY EX? Forgiveness is a basic element in premarital or remarital preparation. One of the best examples of forgiveness is the story of Joseph in Genesis 50. Joseph's brothers have sold him into slavery. Now he rules Egypt, and they have come begging for food in a famine. Does Joseph grin and say, "Payback time!"? Clearly, the brothers expect the worst treatment from him. Read Genesis 50:19-20 appearing in the margin to examine Joseph's model of forgiveness:

Catch that phrase, "Am I in the place of God?" Some of us act that way toward our exes, particularly when they have deeply hurt us. Some of us imagine an ex crawling on hand and knees and confessing, "I was wrong . . .."

In the model prayer, Jesus had a severe word of warning in Matthew 6:15: "But if you do not forgive men their sins, your Father will not forgive your sins." The people we're to forgive definitely include our exes. Sometimes, we think or insist we have forgiven our exes, but it was only surface-level forgiveness. You need to ask: Have I really forgiven my ex?

✎ **Ask yourself, "OK, have I really forgiven my ex?" Answer below.**

_____

_____

_____

This also means you have to ask, "Has the one I am marrying—if previously married—forgiven his/her ex, as well as my ex?" Bitterness toward an ex can spill over to a new spouse. That is no way to start a marriage. Even if reconciliation was not possible in your case and you were unable to put your marriage back together, you still can reconcile with your ex so that you forgive your ex and arrive at the point in which you can treat each other in a Christ-honoring way.

QUESTION 2: HAVE YOU FORGIVEN YOURSELF? You may believe you are only minimally responsible for the breakup of your marriage, but you still need to forgive yourself. If you have not wrestled with the reflective work of what you could have/should have done to save the marriage, you must do it before you can make a new relationship work.

People don't build a house on a vacant lot or in a secluded spot in the woods without preparing the site. That can be lots of work, but it is necessary.

Don't be afraid. Am I in the place of God? You intended to harm me, but God intended it for good to accomplish what is now being done.

–Genesis 50:19-20

It's not the 10 percent of the iceberg above the waterline that sinks the ship It's the 90 percent below. So it is with the "icebergs" lurking in the path of a second marriage.

Forgiving yourself is part of preparing for God's future. On the other hand, some of us have been too tough on ourselves. We have overblown our failures and magnified our inadequacies as a spouse.

How can we forgive ourselves? Simply, ask God to forgive. Some of us will need a friend to help us get rid of our load.

✎ **Repeat the prayer that appears below. Fill in the blanks where necessary:**

O God, I want You to forgive me for my failures as a spouse. I want to own-up to You for what I did. I want to own up to what I did not do. I have overstated my ex's failures and sins. I have demanded full payment for his/her offenses against me, my children, my dreams. Thank You for hearing me and for forgiving me. Father, give me as much courage to forgive _____ as You have forgiven me. Amen.

Forgiving your ex and forgiving yourself are big tasks. Don't be surprised if in a few days, weeks, months, some new items "arrive" to be forgiven.

QUESTION 3: HAS ENOUGH TIME LAPSED FOR HEALING AND RECONCILIATION? You need time to emotionally, spiritually, financially, and physically heal from the draining aspects of a divorce before you begin a new relationship. In fact, a premature relationship could be the worst possible thing for you. It could start you on the path to a second divorce.

How much time? A lot. If he/she is pressuring you or is impatient, you'd better ask, "What's the hurry?" The Holy Spirit needs time to work. Forgiveness cannot always be instant. Some forgiveness, to be genuine, takes time. You need time to deal with the issues that led to the "I want a divorce!" in the first place.

You need time for reconciliation. By reconciliation I do not mean necessarily that you go back to the spouse—even though with God's help that can occur. When people begin to recognize the hardness of their hearts, they can work to save their marriages. Before you consider remarriage—and even if you believe that you are free under the Scriptures to remarry—I encourage you to again examine your heart to determine whether you have done everything possible to help a reconciliation to occur in the marriage that you may think is over. Divorce is not an easy way to escape problems, and Christians should be committed to working out problems in the marriage. (See the verse appearing in the margin.)

> To the married I give this command (not I, but the Lord); a wife (spouse) must not separate from her husband. But if she does, she must remain unmarried or else be reconciled to her husband.
>
> 1 Corinthians 7:11

But even if the marriage cannot be saved, the active hostilities can end. David Seamands wrote, "People must allow themselves sufficient time to be able to make a free choice. This is so they don't bury the hurt, garbage, and wounds of the first marriage under a second marriage. Whatever the time is, it has to be when they're able to say, 'I'm over it. I can accept things as they are. I'm free to make a choice.' To me that takes a minimum of a year or two. Probably two."[19]

QUESTION 4: DOES UNFINISHED BUSINESS FROM THE FIRST MARRIAGE EXIST? You may not have the remains of a first spouse in a cardboard box, but what do you have in your possession? In your memory?

✎ **Below answer these questions.**

1. Have you kept your end of the divorce decree? _____

2. Are your child-support and/or alimony payments up to date? _____

3. Are you on good or tense terms with your ex? _____

4. If not on good terms, what have you done to lessen the hostilities? _____

_____

5. Can you say your ex's name without emotional reaction? _____

6. Are you on good terms with your children? _____

7. Have you forgiven your ex? _____

Unfinished business

The unfinished business may not be simply between you and your ex. How have your children reacted to the emotional, relational, and economic implications of the divorce? If you remarry and start another "family," how will you keep your financial and emotional responsibilities for your first family with integrity? If money is tight, who will suffer: first or second family?

✎ **Take a moment to do an inventory. What are the items of unfinished business in your life? What actions would be necessary to resolve them?**

Unfinished business: _____

_____

What I could do to resolve: _____

_____

Unfinished business from a first marriage has a way of getting moved to the front burner in a remarriage.

QUESTION 5: HOW WILL MY REMARRIAGE AFFECT OTHERS? Your decision to marry impacts a lot of people. Like a pebble being tossed into a pond, it sets off lots of ripples.

✎ **In the space below list by name and relationships those who will be impacted.**

Affected Negatively   Affected Positively

_____   _____

_____   _____

_____   _____

_____   _____

Your ex(es) and children deserve the courtesy of being informed about your plans/intent to remarry. Your ex or children do not have veto power over your decision to remarry, but you do need to give everyone time to get accustomed to the idea. If your children have fantasies of your getting back together with their mom or dad and you unexpectedly burst their bubble with a remarriage, expect major repercussions.

QUESTION 6: WHAT ABOUT THE TIMING? Are you short-circuiting the healing process by a premature second marriage?

✎ **Below answer these questions about the timing of a second marriage.**

1. Is someone rushing me into a second marriage? _____

2. Is this remarriage proof that I am over the divorce? _____

3. Am I on "the rebound"? _____

4. Am I in a race with my ex to see who can remarry first? _____

5. To what degree does money influence my desire for remarriage? _____

_____

6. To what degree does my desire for sex prompt my desire to remarry?

_____

7. What prevents me from postponing remarriage? _____

_____

A person does not build a structure on freshly-poured concrete. Concrete requires time to set-up. The same thing is true for the foundations for a second marriage.

Weekly Work

⟼ **Repeat the affirmation appearing at left.**

I am learning that the tragedies of life can be fertilizer for tomorrow's dream because I am an M.I.P. (miracle-in-progress).

DAY 5

Today's objective:
I will continue to study solid questions before I remarry.

Asking the Right Questions

QUESTION 7: IS REMARRIAGE GOD'S BEST FOR ME?
We should base the decision to remarry on the same conditions as the traditional wedding ceremony requires for a first wedding. God instituted marriage, and we should enter into it—
• Advisedly;
• Reverently;
• Discreetly;
• In the fear of God.

In the space to the right of each term just listed, explain what you think the term means. Be prepared to share your explanations with the group.

Beside *advisedly*, you may have written that this means well thought-out, or carefully considered. Beside *reverently* you may have written respectfully—showing respect both for God and for other people. You may have said that *discreetly* means showing good judgment, and you may have said that *in the fear of God* means honoring God, to the point of seeking His will in the decision to remarry. As a way of determining if remarriage in general or this particular remarriage specifically is God's best for you—ask how many of these four conditions have been/are being met. Consider these two couples' stories:

John and Mary's story

John has been divorced about four months, but it was "love at first sight" when he met Mary. On his third date with Mary, John brought up the subject of remarriage. At the moment he is unemployed, but he is sure he will find a job soon. Mary never has been married. She is 36 and really wants children; John has two boys from the first marriage but hasn't seen them since the divorce. John and Mary plan to marry in two months.

 Evaluate this relationship on the basis of the four criteria. Explain why John and Mary are or are not entering into this remarriage—

Advisedly? _____
Reverently?_____
Discreetly? _____
In the fear of God? _____

Beth and David's story

Beth and David met while each was going through divorce; mutual friends introduced them. Beth's husband left her for a friend, and Beth, a single parent with sons ages three and five, inherited most of the bills. The children are a handful, and her ex rarely comes up with any money for her and the boys. David has four grown children; his marriage ended after 22 years. David never has been much of a church person; Beth has been active in her local church but has been reluctant to tell anyone in the church about her relationship with David for fear they would disapprove.

 Evaluate this relationship on the basis of the four criteria. Explain why Beth and David are or are not entering into this remarriage—

Advisedly? _____
Reverently? _____
Discreetly? _____
In the fear of God? _____

> *Do I wish to seek what I see as my best plan for my life, or will I attempt to reorder my life in accordance with what I think may be God's best plan for my life?*

John Splinter wrote: "There are always consequences when one chooses to live outside God's best plan. Perhaps the most difficult part of this discussion is understanding that remarriage might *not* be God's best plan for the divorced person. . . . At this point, then, the question becomes: Do I wish to seek what I see as *my* best plan for my life, or will I attempt to reorder my life in accordance with what I think may be God's best plan for my life?"[20]

God may be saying "no" to a particular remarriage or to the timing of a remarriage rather than "no" to the idea of remarriage. He may have something more or something special in mind, for down the road—for later.

Congratulations on completing your study of the nine agendas of *A Time for Healing*. As you conclude your study you may want to refer back to the section, "Facing the Future," on page 98 as you consider the next steps of growth you take in your healing process. May God go with you on the journey!

> I am learning that the tragedies of life can fertilize tomorrow's dream because I am an M.I.P. (miracle-in-progress).

Weekly Work

➠ Repeat aloud three times this week's memory verse.

➠ Repeat the affirmation appearing in the margin.

Notes

[1]Lenore J. Weitzman, *The Divorce Revolution*, (New York: Free Press, 1985), 204.

[2]Ibid.

[3]H. Wayne House, "The Bible and Divorce: Three Views," *Discipleship Journal*, Issue 75: (May/June 1993), 33. (For a more complete treatment of these issues, see H. Wayne House, *Divorce and Remarriage: Four Christian Views*. (Downers Grove, IL: Inter-Varsity Press, 1990).

[4]Ibid., 33-34.

[5]Baptist Sunday School Board, *Corporate Editorial Manual*, "Guidelines for Dealing with Family Issues," 5-19

[6]Larry Richards, *Remarriage: A Healing Gift*, (Dallas: Word, 1990), 18.

[7]Frank Stagg, *Matthew-Mark*, vol. 8 of *The Broadman Bible Commentary*, (Nashville: Broadman, 1969), 188.

[8]T. Miles Bennett, *Malachi*, Vol. 7 of *The Broadman Bible Commentary*, (Nashville: Broadman, 1972), 387.

[9]Stagg, 187.

[10]Richards, 103.

[11]House, 39.

[12]Ibid.

[13]John P. Splinter, *The Complete Recovery Handbook*, (Grand Rapids, MI: Zondervan, 1992), 189-190.

[14]House, 40.

[15]Ibid., 37.

[16]John F. Walvoord and Roy B. Zuck, *The Bible Knowledge Commentary*, (Wheaton: Victor, 1983), 64.

[17]House, 37.

[18]Chuck Shepherd. "News of the Weird." (Universal Press Syndicate), *PitchWeekly*, 24 March 1994, 38.

[19]David Seamands, "An Interview with David Seamands: How Long Should a Pastor Encourage Someone to Pursue Reconciliation?" *Single Adult Ministry Journal*, ed. Jerry Jones, (Colorado Springs: Navpress, 1991), 259.

[20]Splinter, 196.